Libraries
in the
USSR

Libraries
in the
USSR

edited by Simon Francis

LINNET BOOKS & CLIVE BINGLEY LTD

TRANSLATED FROM RUSSIAN AND FIRST PUBLISHED 1971 IN UK
BY CLIVE BINGLEY LTD
THIS EDITION SIMULTANEOUSLY PUBLISHED IN THE USA
BY LINNET BOOKS, AN IMPRINT OF SHOE STRING PRESS INC,
995 SHERMAN AVENUE, HAMDEN, CONNECTICUT 06514
PRINTED IN GREAT BRITAIN
0-208-01059-9

CONTENTS

ACKNOWLEDGEMENTS: Thanks must go first and foremost to the National Lending Library for Science and Technology under whose Russian Translation Scheme the basic translation was made, and whose collection of report literature enabled the supplementary bibliography to be compiled, very largely as a result of personal examination of the items it contains. My colleagues at the North-Western Polytechnic School of Librarianship, and in particular the members of its library staff, cheerfully suffered the trials of an editor, as did the staff of the University of London and Aslib libraries.

NOTE: Unlike other national studies in the present series, this volume does not contain a map showing state boundaries and principal cities and towns. This is because the enormous area encompassed by the USSR cannot be adequately represented on the page-size of this book, and students are therefore referred to an atlas for the location of places described in the text.

INTRODUCTION

This book is a translation of a collection of papers published, in commemoration of the fiftieth anniversary of the Revolution, late in 1967 as a special issue of the Soviet journal *Biblioteki SSSR*.

My purpose in editing this translation has been twofold. The first is to make available a body of information about Soviet librarianship. It may be argued that the professional literature is already replete and should not be increased without very good cause. However, while some areas certainly do suffer from an overabundance of literature, the comparative study of librarianship in general and of Soviet librarianship in particular, in spite of a welcome growth of interest, has not yet reached this stage. Moreover, the bulk of commonly known literature is restricted either to being written from a Soviet viewpoint or by being in Russian. In reaching a wider audience than the original of this text could hope to do, a greater knowledge of Soviet librarianship should result.

The second aim is closely related to the first. If we find some of the writing in this collection exaggerated, it is still of importance to examine it and attempt to understand the reasons and climate which produce it. We may not agree with some of the implications that the authors draw from the factual material presented, but we cannot dismiss it as external propaganda. This is how *they* see *themselves* and how they wish to be seen by their colleagues and compatriots. Nevertheless, I have felt it necessary to edit the original quite considerably, not in any way to distort the narrative, but because the sheer clutter of patriotic and ideological sentiment in which much of the writing is clothed acts as a distracting and irritating gloss upon the information being imparted. In this connection it is important to note that the first three sections of the original text—the preface ' The Leninist program for library service to the public ', chapter I ' First measures of the Soviet Government in the field of library development ', and chapter II ' The resolution of the Central Executive Committee of the USSR " On library affairs in the Soviet Union " (1934) ' have all been amalgamated and condensed into the first chapter of this translation. Readers should accept the natural pride of each contributor in the developments described, and thus allow deletion of the innumerable, and often purple, accolades to the 1917 revolution and its after effects.

For this reason the supplementary bibliography included with this translation has been strictly limited to works written by Russian librarians for their colleagues. From this it is possible to build up a very representative and revealing picture of the published Soviet viewpoint on Soviet literature. For source material on the USSR library situation in the immediate post-revolutionary period, readers are referred to *Lenin, Krupskaia & libraries* edited by S Simsova (Bingley 1968) in which a number of early government decrees are given in translation.

The picture, I suggest, shows very clearly the tremendous need for improvement that the 1917 revolution revealed and the subsequent efforts to fulfil that need. We may again disagree in our viewpoints on the evidence presented and on the roles played, but we cannot dismiss the earnestness of the endeavour. What does stand out is the almost total lack of comparison with other countries. The references are copious, but all save a handful are to Soviet sources. Those of us who find our efforts stimulated through comparison with others may wonder at this chauvinistic approach.

July 1970   SIMON FRANCIS

I EARLY LIBRARY DEVELOPMENT

It is clear that long before the revolution Lenin had been thinking and writing about the need to harness libraries to the struggle for mass education and political awareness. Several early papers are quoted to show how Lenin appreciated the power of libraries and how he looked to the progress made by libraries in Western Europe and the United States as an ideal to be followed. Frequent evidence is given of the extremely poor state of library development in pre- and immediate post-revolutionary Russia. Libraries were non-existent in many areas and where they did exist were starved of funds, space and qualified staff.

The Revolution and the new control of education and library affairs was not welcomed universally, particularly by the senior staffs of the larger libraries and the Ministry of Education. There are accounts of opposition and even sabotage resulting from the dismissal of reactionary staff, as well as the disappearance of papers and money from ministries in an attempt to hamper the work of the new people's commissars.

Measures were taken early after the revolution to nationalise all libraries and bookstocks, and to place them under the control of local commissars. Collections, sometimes of considerable size, which were formerly in private hands were thus made available to everyone. There was indignation at those who fled abroad, in some cases taking valuable materials with them. The unrest of the civil war had resulted in the plunder and destruction of many of the private collections and it became necessary to establish local and regional stores to ensure the safety of bookstocks. The earlier total enforcement of nationalisation was modified to allow those who required books as working tools to retain their own collections. Evidence is given that Lenin himself intervened on behalf of ' P I Surkov, a former deputy state councillor of Kostroma Province,' who had complained about the requisitioning of his library.

In passing a law promoting the creation of a single centralised library system in the country, the Soviet of People's Commissars was giving expression to Lenin's belief in the need for the widest possible use of books and reading by the public. One early measure was to

1*

register all libraries and to set up an inspectorate to ensure conformity with standards and with policy decisions decreed by the Central Library Commission of the People's Commissariat for Education. Very considerable efforts were made to redistribute the stocks which had been requisitioned, so that a much larger area of the country could be served by libraries. Even during the civil war which followed the revolution the Red Army set up reading rooms and small collections of books and pamphlets in several areas. Rural areas had been particularly poorly served before the revolution and considerable effort and resources were now expended in providing an adequate level of service to the peasants. At present almost three-quarters of all public libraries are situated in country areas. At first villages set up their own club libraries and reading rooms, but these were later incorporated into the public library network, after being replaced by mobile and travelling libraries operated from nearby towns and cities.

In addition to the establishment of many scientific and technical libraries in manufacturing and research works, attention was also given to the provision of library facilities available to the general workers employed within the factories and centres. This tremendous increase in the number of libraries and in the quality of their services necessitated the establishment of adequate training in library techniques. Full-time and evening courses were set up in a number of places and training at several levels was offered. Postgraduate studies are now possible in Moscow and Leningrad.

The wide ranging political changes during this period gave rise to an extensive reorientation in the cultural environment. Such reorientation was so far reaching that in 1934, at the Seventeenth Congress of the Communist Party, legislation was passed which was to determine the course of Soviet library development for many years hence.

Previously, and despite the social changes prevalent, the peasant population had remained almost totally illiterate. To combat this a program of extensive adult education was introduced together with campaigns to constitute library service in factories, farms, and other places of work and recreation. In spite of these considerable efforts the standard of library service was still found to be severely inadequate, due mainly to a lack of qualified staff, and to the overwhelming emphasis which had been placed on adult education which had consequently diverted attention from library development. To remedy these deficiencies measures were introduced, from 1932 onwards, both to popularise the libraries with the majority of the people, and to develop an extensive network of regional libraries. It was suggested at the 1934 Congress that responsibility for the control of library development, staff training, and book acquisition should be delegated to the Commissariat for education in each republic, and that the post of a supervising library inspector should be introduced into each region. Improvements were also suggested in the library services to rural populations as well as a new appraisal of general methods of book acquisition.

The urgent need for a higher proportion of qualified personnel was catered for by an increase and extension of the training facilities avaliable to student librarians. A higher expenditure on library development was also advocated.

The resolutions of the 1934 Congress can be seen as an important turning point in the development of Soviet library affairs. Systems of state library direction were introduced and completely new methods of library organisation were brought into practice. Renewed and concentrated efforts were made to bring the public into the libraries, and further recommendations were also put forward regarding the establishment of regional libraries in each and every district. Reactions to the resolutions were not immediate; a census carried out eight months after the Congress showed that state libraries were still inadequate compared to the public libraries, and that though the demand for technical information was high the research libraries were very seldom used. Nevertheless after the 1934 Congress the library situation was improved greatly, and the changes made, after acting on the recommendations of the Congress, were to radically increase the efficiency of library service in Russia.

Throughout the period directly following the Congress great advances were made in book acquisition procedures. Territorial and executive committees were compulsorily required to render funds available to libraries for book purchase, while at the same time libraries were allowed an increasing independence in their choice of stock. Regional acquisition departments were now also being regarded as active and essential aids to the libraries, and their sphere of influence was rapidly widening. Library workers and users were consulted about their requirements, and their comments were noted and acted upon. Arrangements were made which required publishers to allocate a proportion of each edition for the sole use of the libraries, and to produce reviews of their publications for specific library distribution. Problems concerning organised restocking were also given extensive attention.

The entire system of library education was now challenged, and became the subject of critical discussion. To help overcome many of the long standing inefficiencies in this area the intake of students into special and higher educational institutes was substantially increased, and an independent faculty at the Leningrad Krupskaia Institute was inaugurated. New methods of tuition in librarianship were introduced and were augmented by newly written, more up to date, student text books. Conferences began to feature predominantly and played a significant part in the planning of student curricula.

The years from the seventeenth Congress of the Communist Party in 1934 to 1937 can, as stated previously, easily be seen as a period of major achievement in the Soviet library movement. Though many of the libraries were utilised predominantly as political forums and centres of propaganda the extensive advances made in providing an efficient library service to the masses cannot be overlooked. The problems of administration at such a time, over such an area, and in such circumstances would seem, at first sight, insurmountable, and it is solely to the determination of a number of dedicated librarians that the infinite credit for overcoming such difficulties is due.

II STATE LIBRARIES OF THE SOVIET REPUBLICS
by O S CHUBAR'YAN

The creation of large central state libraries serving each of the Union republics is related to the considerable library development achieved since the introduction of Soviet administration. The republic libraries became important cultural centres, and the following examination of their development and characteristics is extremely instructive for the whole library network of the country as well as for the Soviet library movement in general.

THE CREATION OF THE REPUBLIC LIBRARY NETWORK
During the course of their development the republic libraries have overcome many complex difficulties. A large number of libraries, being founded prior to the revolution, inherited the bookstocks of the large, long established libraries such as those of Georgia, founded in 1846, the Ukraine, founded in 1866 and in Uzbekistan, founded in 1870. In this present account of library development it is only examples of this type of library that will be considered. The majority of the libraries which later formed the basis of the republic library network did not warrant state recognition as central library institutes in pre-revolutionary times due to their being regarded as not entering into any form of cultural or educational activities. It is obvious therefore that the republic libraries were established solely as the result of the Soviet system.

In the early post-revolutionary period the Soviet government strove to ally the progress of the general state libraries to the development of a socialist doctrine in areas of culture and economics, and it was by these efforts that even during the first years of Soviet administration the ambition to create central libraries in each of the republics was, to a large extent, fulfilled. Some measure of the government's efforts can be gauged when it is realised that shortly after the proclamation of Soviet rule in Latvia, in 1919, a decree was issued which contained clauses relating to the organisation of a Latvian central library,[1] four years later measures being introduced to establish a republic state central library.[2] Central libraries were also established in the Azerbaijan republic (1923)[3] and in the Tajik republic (1929).[4]

The ever increasing requirements of the economy, science and culture constantly determined not only the wide range of republic library activities, but also the high rate at which they developed. The following figures will give some indication of this progress[5]: the bookstocks held by fourteen republic libraries in 1966 amounted to 38·8 million volumes. When compared with the all-Union census of 1934, showing a stock 4·8 million books held, this figure indicates an increase of some 800 percent. In 1966 four libraries stocked from 1 to 2 million books each, seven libraries held from 2 to 3 million volumes, and three libraries possessed more than 3 million volumes each.

The numbers of readers using republic libraries has increased steadily, there being in 1947, 75·6 thousand, and in 1965, 361·6 thousand. In 1947, the number of loans amounted to 4·2 million volumes, and by 1965 it had increased by more than four times, reaching 17·1 million volumes.

The varied bibliographical work of republic libraries had also increased greatly; in 1965 ten libraries alone issuing some five hundred bibliographic reference books and preparing a hundred bibliographic, scientific and systematic guides.

The last six to seven years have been especially fruitful in the development of the republic libraries. The efforts to act according to the resolution of the central committee of the Communist Party ' On the state and measures for improvement of library affairs in the country ' (1959) promoted a wide increase in the level and scope of their activities. In comparison with 1959, the stocks of republic libraries have increased by 14 million volumes, the number of readers by 150 thousand, the attendance by 1·5 million people and the book issue by 8 million volumes.

On the suggestions of the 1959 resolution, the material and technical resources of republic libraries were combined and many new buildings for libraries were utilised, examples being those of the Moldavian SSR (1960), the Lithuanian SSR (1961), the Azerbaijan SSR (1962) and the Kirghiz SSR (1963). In 1961 and 1962, great extensions were also added to the library buildings of the Belorussian SSR and the Uzbek SSR, and in 1967 and 1968, construction of the Turkmen and Kazakh SSR libraries was completed.

A short time after the Lithuanian republic library obtained more

14

modern premises (after being transferred from Kaunas to Vilnius), the number of readers increased from 9 thousand to 33 thousand, the annual number of visits increasing from 83 thousand to 520 thousand, and the annual issues from 480 thousand to 1·1 million volumes. In the first two years after the move of the Kirghiz SSR library to new premises, the number of its readers increased from 16 thousand to 46 thousand and the number of visits in a year increased from 194 thousand to 440 thousand, the annual book issue increasing from 750 thousand to 2 million. It is easy to see, therefore, that during the years of Soviet administration the republic libraries grew to such an extent as to become comparable to the largest libraries in many parts of the world.

However progress, after fifty years of republic library development, cannot be shown only by statistics. It is difficult to assess the contribution which the republic libraries have made in the dissemination of scientific and technical information. As an acknowledgement of the extensive activity of the state republic library of the Ukrainian SSR, the Communist Party decorated it, in 1966, with the Order of the Red Banner of Labour.[6] This public recognition of the republic libraries' efforts emphasises the high importance placed by the government on their wide accessibility to all strata of society, as well as on their essential service to readers in the more specialised fields of scientific information work. In spite of the growth of specialised libraries (in scientific, technical, agricultural and higher educational institutions) in the republics, the scale of activity of the republic libraries has consistently expanded.

In January 1967 the *Exemplary manual for state libraries of the Union Republics* was endorsed by the Ministry of Culture.[7] This was the first document defining the form and functions of state republic libraries as seen on an all-Union scale. In it not only is the experience gained during the fifty years since their formation outlined, but also the nature and direction of their further development. The *Exemplary manual* assists in showing which important scientific works are available in republic libraries, and in particular, analyses the characteristics of each library, and describing the general, national and specific activities carried by them.

There has not so far been any single paper outlining the experience gained by the republic libraries in the field of specialist literature. The filling of this gap, itself one of the most urgent problems in Soviet library science, would eliminate anomalies which are known to exist in current practice.

The principles of stock selection in the republic libraries, the course of their wider use and the prospects for the development of libraries as information centres must be seriously studied. The rationalisation of their use and the implementation of standard practices which will secure uniform conditions in their work, awaits completion. The investigation of all these problems is impossible without the active participation of the republic libraries, and without the development of sociological methods for examining readers and the effectiveness of library and bibliographical services.

CHARACTERISTICS OF LIBRARIES IN THE REPUBLICS

The *Exemplary manual* indicates that the libraries of the republics in their present form fulfil the following functions: 1) as state book stores of importance to the whole republic; 2) as the largest public library in each Union republic; 3) as the leading biblio-graphical institution of the republic, and 4) as the scientific methods centre for the library network of every Union republic. These functions indicate the complexity of the problems and solutions for a system of providing library service to the population.

The republic libraries are counted among the national libraries of the Soviet Union. This concept, widespread in foreign library science, applies to the largest libraries in the country which play the role of state (national) book depositories and enjoy the rights of an official state library institution.

During the years of Soviet administration, the concept of ' a national library ' changed and has been extended as new implications became apparent. It is not an exclusive depository of national literature but an active and widely accessible library institution with many complex functions. In the state library system, the republic libraries occupy a leading position, acting as state book repositories and as centres at which all scientific, industrial and cultural material, published within each republic, is freely available.

In the formation and development of republic libraries (and similarly the republic book chambers), the important and complex problem of defining the concepts of ' the stock of national litera-

16

ture' and 'the national library' has been practically and theoretically solved. Some library scientists and bibliographers interpreted these concepts very widely. Thus as criteria for defining 'the stock of national literature' and 'national bibliography', they named the place of issue of the printed work, the language in which it was printed, the nationality of the author (independently of his place of residence), and the regional (of the given republic) relevance of the contents of the printed material, independently of the place of its issue.[8] Experience showed that attempts to combine all these criteria (for example, in a bibliographical index) or indeed to exaggerate the significance of one of the formal criteria (for example, the language of the printed work, or the author's place of origin), when taken without due regard to the historical characteristics of the development of the nation, eliminated the possibility of assessing printed material from the point of view of the Leninist doctrine.

The experience of republic libraries and book chambers demonstrated that the practice of applying these leading criteria to the choosing of publications for the stocks of national literature and national bibliography could be correctly and scientifically established. This experience also proved that advantages ensue from using the territorial criterion for the choice of works in the national literature and bibliography of the Union republics, bringing together the literature, printed drawings, maps and audio visual materials published in the territory of the national state.

Certain exceptions can be made from the above rule, conditioned by the varying types of historical and socialistic background of the people. For example, while the different nations of former Tsarist Russia were establishing their socialist statehood, their books were issued in various countries and naturally must be included in the concept of 'the national stock'. During the second world war, when the territory of a number of Union republics was temporarily occupied, their publishing activity was carried out in other Union republics and this production has also supplemented the stocks of national literature. In our opinion, while it is necessary to consider separately books of local lore and character, or publications in the language of each republic, but published outside that republic, it is not advisable to include them in the concept of the 'stocks of the national literature' or the 'national bibliography'.[9]

Stocks of national literature are selected in a wide and varied program by republic libraries. Every republic library now has available a comparatively complete stock of printed works produced within its republic. Thus the stock of national literature in the Karl Marx State Library of the Georgian SSR is reckoned to be about 300 thousand volumes, stocking publications of the Soviet period and also publications reflecting the centuries old history of the nation, beginning with the first Georgian printed books published in 1629 in Rome. The stocks of national literature of other republic libraries have an exclusively cultural value. The systematic and comprehensive selection of the stocks of Soviet national literature is ensured by the compulsory supply of copies of the printed works of the republic, which all republic libraries receive on a daily basis as central library institutions.

The contribution of republic libraries to the development of national bibliography is considerable. In October 1965, the all-Union book chamber, together with the chief library inspection department of the Ministry of Culture and the Lenin State Library, called an all-Union conference and seminar on retrospective bibliography in the national republics, at which the results of this work in the area were described.[10] A very valuable bibliographic guide to the stocks has been compiled by the republic libraries who, in close cooperation with other research libraries and republic book chambers, have produced a fundamental retrospective bibliographic index of national literature, the value of which is difficult to overestimate.[11] The creation of bibliographies of a similar kind forms one of the basic bibliographic tasks of the republic libraries. It is to the credit of the republic libraries of the Belorussian, Kazakh, and Lithuanian SSRs that deficiences in state bibliographic registration of book production have been completely eliminated.

The republic libraries have also fully developed such important areas of work as compiling and distributing bibliographies of literature from each republic, covering its productive and natural resources, economy, history and culture. In solving this problem, the republic libraries have made extensive advances. The relevant stocks of literature, especially the selection of printed works on a given republic issued outside its area, are of considerable value and are widely used both by the general public and research workers. A

18

system of indexes to current and retrospective bibliographic summaries of publications on each republic is now being established.[12] At the present time, in Azerbaijan, Belorussia, Georgia, Latvia, Lithuania, Tajikistan, Turkmenistan, Ukraine, Estonia, sections are included in *Leptopisi pechati* (Chronicles of printed matter) or bibliographies are issued separately in *Respublika v pechati SSSR* (The republic in print in the USSR) or *Respublika v pechati SSR i zarubezhnykh sotsialisticheskikh stran* (The republic in print in USSR and foreign socialist countries). But the necessary uniformity has not yet been achieved in the compilation of such indexes, and many problems (especially in the principles of selecting literature and the correlation of these indexes with state bibliographic registration) continue to remain open for discussion.

All the republic libraries actively promote regional information, but at present they organise work with the literature relating to the republic in different ways. Thus, in some libraries complex regional divisions (indeed even their names differ) are created in which different stocks are concentrated. In a number of cases these stocks include not only literature relating to the republic but also all the national literature and all books in the language of that republic independent of their place of publication. This practice can hardly be justified. If it is felt necessary to separate stocks and set up special divisions, then they should only be divisions of a regional character and must be limited to matters about the republic. We maintain that republic libraries which do not set up separate and complex structural subdivisions, act rightly and solve many of the problems inherent in this type of work by bibliographic methods and also by means of the organisation of special reading rooms (with small subsidiary reference libraries) for differing service to readers based on the main stocks of the library.[13]

To sum up, through their efforts the scientific and cultural achievements of the USSR become available to the people of each individual republic, and the experience of individual republics is utilised on an all-Union scale. To publicise the advances of socialist development in the conditions of the multi-nation Soviet state forms the main task of library service to the people.

The problem of cultural advancement was initially solved by the acquisition of book stocks, which included not only national literature but also the basic printed work of all the nations of the Soviet Union in all branches of knowledge, selected according to a wide program. The compulsory purchase of the main publications in Russian created a simple basis for the systematic formation of their book stocks, and for the centralisation of the most important sources of scientific and cultural achievements gained throughout the USSR. Book exchange between the republic libraries serves the same purpose.

Republic libraries now comprise the most complete library stock within each republic, reflecting the development of science, technology and culture in the whole Soviet Union and ensuring that a wide variety of enquiries from all sections of the population can be satisfied.

In the cultural, educational, and scientific information work of republic libraries, the spreading of such forms of cultural enrichment as comprehensive bibliographic handbooks of various types continually increases. Systematic generalisation of experience in the compilation of such handbooks is at present an unsolved problem of Soviet bibliography.

Bibliographies of recommended titles, acting as a means of promoting books and for guiding readers, play an important role in the dissemination of culture. Republic libraries make an invaluable contribution to the production of such bibliographies.[14] One aspect of these bibliographies, published by republic libraries, is their national character; nine out of ten of all lists being devoted to problems of the development within each of the Union republics concerned. A considerable proportion of the lists are compiled in the language of the national republic. This makes them generally accessible and helps to publicise widely, not only literature on the given republic, but also all of the most important achievements of other republics.

For example, in 1966 alone, the state library of the Kirghiz SSR issued twenty one bibliographical handbooks recommending literature on science, technology, industry and public life, in which not only Kirghiz national literature was widely covered but also the most important books in Russian and the languages of the other republics of the USSR. The republic libraries of Azerbaijan, Georgia,

20

Latvia SSRs and others have undertaken considerable work in the production of bibliographies.

REPUBLIC LIBRARIES AND THE SYSTEM OF SCIENTIFIC AND TECHNICAL INFORMATION

An important part of the activity of republic libraries is active participation in making widely known the scientific and technical achievements of our state. The main growth areas of this type of library have been in library and bibliographic help to science and industry.

The Communist Party of the Soviet Union, in its program documents and in the resolutions of the Twenty Third Congress of the Communist Party, paid special attention to perfecting the scientific and technical information system. The first priority for the republic libraries is to give practical assistance to scholars and specialists to enable them to become acquainted with the latest achievements of science and technology with the least expenditure of effort and time. Full use of the extensive stocks of the republic libraries depends upon the realisation of this task.

It should be mentioned that during the years of Soviet rule, substantial successes have been achieved in the answering of inquiries dealing with science and industry in the republics by means of books and bibliographies, many scholars and specialists making regular use of republic libraries. Thus, in 1965, the number of readers of this group in the Azerbaijan library amounted to 10 thousand, in Georgia to 8·1 thousand, in Kirghiz and Moldavia to 7·1 thousand each, in Kazakh to 5·3 thousand and in Uzbekistan to about 4 thousand. In the last ten to fifteen years, the number of readers (scholars and specialists) in almost all republic libraries has doubled. Special extensions housing, for example, reading rooms, foke lore libraries or bibliographical sections, were established to serve the needs of interested readers. General catalogues and retrospective national bibliographies were also used to satisfy the growing number of complex inquiries from specialist readers. Display work is increasingly devoted to the supply of information for these categories of readers. The practice of reading rooms, where, for example, weekly or every ten days an exhibition is presented of recent literature acquired by the library, deserves to

21

be widely followed. These reading rooms have proved to be very popular, and provide a means of attracting scholars and specialists to the library. It is significant that republic libraries very often hold prominent exhibitions of literature on current topics in the sciences and industry. Many exhibitions are organised outside the library, at scientific conferences and various meetings, as well as at various undertakings, research establishments, and institutions. The efficiency of the exhibition as a means of information is thereby enhanced.

Republic libraries widely practice methods of individual and collective dissemination of information based on surveys of current literature. Specific requests come from Party, Soviet and economic organisations, leading undertakings and research establishments in the republic. For example, the state library of the Kazakh SSR passes information to almost three hundred organisations in the republic. It is possible to quote many other similar examples. At the same time the level of development of information work achieved by republic libraries is no longer satisfactory and lags behind the modern requirements of science and industry. The great potentialities of the libraries (their stocks, subsidiary reference material, and qualified staff) are obviously insufficiently used. It is necessary to increase their role as information centres and to broaden their activities in areas of science and industry.

The number of scientists and economists who make use of the republic libraries is an insignificant proportion of the total number of readers; at the beginning of 1965, for example, eight specified libraries had the following percentages of scientists and specialists among their readers: in the libraries of the Uzbek and Armenian SSRs 10 percent each; in the libraries of the Turkmen and Kirghiz SSRs 15 to 20 percent, and only in the libraries of the Georgian, Azerbaijan and Moldavian SSRs did this figure exceed 30 percent. It can be seen that far from all the scientific workers and specialists make frequent use of the republic libraries, their rich book stocks and reference and bibliographic equipment. This is also confirmed by the fact that in spite of the invariable increase in the number of book issues, the proportion of industrial literature in the total book issue remains relatively low. For example, in the libraries of the Central Asian and Kazakhstan SSRs in 1965, the issue of technical literature remained at the level of only 10·7 percent, and agricultural literature at 2·9 percent of the total. In the state library of the Armenian SSR, the proportion of technical and agricultural literature in the total book issue in recent years amounted to 13 to 14 percent. This situation is, unfortunately, typical in many republic libraries.

The task which stands out very clearly in front of the republic libraries is to change the ratio between the different groups of readers and to obtain a majority of scholars and specialists, and consequently an increase in the use and turnover of the fundamental stocks of scientific and industrial value. This cannot be achieved by the exclusion of certain groups of the population from the readership and the narrowing of the cultural and educational functions of the libraries. The solution to this complex problem lies in differentiation of service, in preferential development and the perfecting of information and methods of work for the assistance of science and industry. To sum up, there must be rapid widening in the role of republic libraries as general research libraries as well as centres of library and bibliographic information.

On 29 November 1966, the Council of Ministers of the USSR took a resolution ' On the state system of scientific and technical information.'[15] In it precise measures for the realisation of the resolution of the Twenty Third Congress were outlined and the task of creating a highly efficient system of scientific and technical information in the country, relevant to the new economic conditions and the increasing demands of scholars, engineers, inventors in industry and workers in state organisations was mapped out. Branch information services form the basis of this system; they are integral links in the control of the national economy, by which assistance is provided for the successful completion of production plans and scientific and technical progress.[16] Scientific, technical and special libraries are considered in this resolution as links in the state system of research and technical information, and a significant role is played by them in spreading the latest scientific, technological and industrial achievements. The Council of Ministers of the USSR laid before the Ministry of Culture the task of perfecting the scientific information work of the large general libraries and their being equipped with modern technical resources. In this way, the charac-

23

teristics and perspectives of a new stage in the development of information service were determined. In connection with this it is important to point out ways of developing republic libraries in order to fulfil their role in the solution of the urgent tasks encountered in information service to science and industry.

First of all, cooperation between republic libraries and scientific and technical information centres is unfortunately not always systematically or scientifically carried out. Only through extensive cooperation can they guarantee a high level of complete and flexible information service to science and industry.

In the area of information dissemination the centres, concentrating mainly on distribution of factual information, contrast with the libraries who attempt to provide scholars and specialists with the most effective means of making use of a world wide selection of informative literature. Republic libraries face two further important tasks which have, as yet, been insufficiently completed. These are the securing of a bibliographical approach to the work of information organisations and the supply of material for abstracting journals and collected works, reviews of the development of science and technology, reports on the achievements of scientific research and also the establishment of information services. These problems are currently being solved by the republic libraries on the basis of close cooperation with information services, on a unified coordinated plan.

The republic libraries contain leading library and bibliographical sections which carry the responsibility for the organisation on a republic scale of book resources for science and industry. As part of their duties as general libraries first precedence is given to library and bibliographic information on the national literature[17] and the literature of the republic, on the interdisciplinary and complex problems of science, technology and on the humanities. The republic libraries not only actively cooperate in the formation and the perfection of the national system of bibliographic publications but also organise the use of the scientific and specialist libraries of the republic in a centralised system of all-Union bibliographical information.

Secondly, there is the organisation of a unified all-republic reference service according to general and specialised reference and in-

24

formation stocks, in order that they should become available to scientists, specialists, industrial concerns, scientific research institutions and government organisations in the republic.

Thirdly, there is coordination and cooperation in the work of scientific and research libraries, the main result of which is the creation of a unified and rational system of library and information service for science and industry in each Union republic.

Let us consider some problems in the further development of information work in republic libraries, resulting from the resolution of the Council of Ministers of the USSR ' On the State system of scientific and technical information '.

REPUBLIC LIBRARIES AND A UNIFIED SYSTEM OF LIBRARY SERVICE FOR SCIENCE AND INDUSTRY

The high rate of scientific and technical progress, the ever decreasing barriers between the sciences and the unprecedented increase in scientific literature, urgently demand the practical implementation of a unified system of library and bibliographic service to scholars and specialists. Very few, if any, libraries can independently satisfy all the requests of science and industry, even when continuously expanding their stocks. Only coordination and cooperation between the scientific and special libraries can provide a reliable basic system of library and information as well as service, and the most effective use of library stocks. If the regional aspect of this problem, for instance, on a republic scale is considered, then it is only possible to solve it successfully on the basis of the republic library in its functional role. It is possible that the principle of unity should be extended, not only over the choice of library stock but also over the whole system of library and information service so that the necessary conditions for the most rational use of the literature collected in scientific and special libraries can be created.

Republic libraries have performed considerable work on the co-ordination of stock acquisition in libraries of different types. However, it must be said that this work has been haphazard and at present does not provide a complete interchange system between stocks of the basic libraries of the republic, to guarantee high quality and comprehensive collections in the most important areas of development in science and industry. Unreasonable duplication is

25

still found in the acquisitions of the major libraries, especially in the proportion of the so called ' unpopular ' literature.

At the present we are working out a practical and unified acquisitions policy for scientific and research libraries in each republic, considering this as the most suitable form of coordination in the selection of stocks. By this means a simpler basis for developing active and efficient scientific and technical information systems in the Union republics will be formed.

Unified and planned acquisition of stocks in the scientific and research libraries of the republic is a complicated task. It is sufficient to say that in the course of implementing the chosen plan, not only will the various organisational and methodological problems have to be solved, but also the remains of narrow departmental views must be overcome. The selection of literature for a series of libraries can then be carried out taking into account a true perspective of its use and noting links with libraries of similar types. This must in fact be a unified plan, clearly differentiating between the character and functions of the stocks of the separate libraries, establishing close cooperation in acquisitions, considering the whole stock on a republic scale. The unified plan is the basis for equal collaboration between the greatest libraries of the Union republics.

Cooperative acquisition of books in scientific and research libraries also assumes the creation of a unified plan of library and bibliographical service to the scholars and specialists in the republic. The combined planning of the bibliographical work among science libraries in the Union republics has proved to be useful experience in this respect.

Each plan for library and bibliographical service has the following objects: 1) the clear assignment of duties in direct service to readers on the basis of wide mutual use of books stocks; 2) the creation and joint use of centralised reference and bibliographic aids, and 3) the coordination of the libraries of the republic in the compilation and issue of current and retrospective bibliographic indexes, union catalogues and other sources of information. It should be mentioned that the experience of the republic libraries in methods of joint planning still await examination and generalisation.

The resolution of the Council of Ministers ' On the state system of scientific and technical information ' on 29 November 1966 also created a very important organisational prerequisite for the practical implementation of a unified system of library and bibliographical service. The inter-departmental commission coordinating the work of scientific and research libraries attached to the state committee of the USSR Council of Ministers for scientific and technical education was given very broad authority. In the Union republics, similar commissions were created which will be guided in their work by a combination of the great central research libraries, especially those of the republics.

REPUBLIC LIBRARIES AND THE PROBLEM OF DEPOSITORY STORAGE
The resolution also stressed the necessity for the formation of libraries with depository storage facilities. This task arises from the co-ordinated plan for stock acquisition in the scientific and research libraries of each Union republic. The stocks of the majority of such libraries, particularly in scientific research institutes, contain only the most frequently required literature. It is not necessary to retain older and less used materials nor those from fringe areas of interest. Such types of material must be concentrated in large libraries which, functioning as storage depositories, make even the most specialist material widely available. At the same time the depositories must not to any extent represent lumber store rooms, ignoring the scientific value of the literature. The stocks must be active and capable of being included in the collections of the great central libraries which are generally available to a large proportion of the public.

To the republic libraries, as the major general library institutions of each republic, are entrusted the functions of a library depository and of a centre for organising a system of depository storage within the republic.

REPUBLIC LIBRARIES AND INTER-LIBRARY RELATIONS IN THE REPUBLIC
In the interests of the most complete and economical supply of books and bibliographies to science and industry it is necessary to extensively reorganise inter-library relations. The experience of many libraries showed that in spite of the considerable overall increase in use, the inter-library system, up till now, mainly satisfies the majority of isolated enquiries. The reconstruction of the inter-

27

library system must first of all be founded on the principle that the system constitutes the basic link in the inter-library utilisation of stocks common to all scientific and research libraries. Secondly, it enters into the cooperative system for dealing with the inquiries of scholars and specialists, and thirdly, works on the principle of a centralised progressive organisation. The republic libraries must negotiate a system of inter-library agreements. This is the foremost task in the establishment of a comprehensive and cooperative library service dealing with the scientific and industrial inquiries in the republic. Only after all local sources for satisfying inquiries on literature have been exhausted should the republic libraries systematically use the stocks of libraries of all-Union status as laid down in the inter-library system.

In connection with long term reconstruction and expansion of the inter-library system, it is very important to plan and to develop on the basis of the latest technical achievements, and to utilise the reliable and constantly active two-way links between republic libraries and the Lenin State Library.

REPUBLIC LIBRARIES AND THE PROBLEM OF UNION CATALOGUES

One task already entrusted to republic libraries, in the resolution ' On the state system of scientific and technical information ', is the creation of a system of union catalogues of the science and special libraries in the Union republics. Reliable experience gained in the republics has been accumulated in the catalogues, which mainly cover national literature. However, the compilation of a regional union catalogue is being put forward as a long term aim.

The implementation of unified plan for the acquisition of stock by scientific and research libraries, and for the formation of depository libraries, demands a different basis of inter-library cooperation from that at present being practised. The significance of printed union catalogues as sources of information is increased when it is realised that they are the means of wide mutual use of the stocks of science and special libraries, as well as the means of perfecting the system of inter-library cooperation. The special value of printed union catalogues is obvious to specialists in agriculture, doctors, teachers and other categories of reader who, being in the provinces, are unable to have easy access to the large libraries. The problem must not only be considered retrospectively, but also currently with the publication of printed union catalogues of recent materials with subsequent cumulations over lengthy periods.

The republic libraries play a major role in the publication of union catalogues. Within the bounds of the unified state system, it is necessary to define the types of union catalogue, the stages in the subsequent solution of this problem, the range of literature included in them, the methods of cooperation in compilation for scientific and research libraries, and to choose and to develop the most effective techniques for the reproduction of such catalogues. In addition problems in the creation of regional union catalogues of foreign publications and of stocks of national literature must be solved.

REPUBLIC LIBRARIES AND THE PROBLEM OF CENTRALISATION OF REFERENCE AND BIBLIOGRAPHIC SERVICE

Experience shows that the most effective and economic centralisation of reference and bibliographic service is that based on the great general libraries. As distinct from specialised libraries, orientated towards the answering of specific professional and industrial inquiries, the reference and bibliographical service of the general library has a more complex character, reflecting the interdisciplinary nature of sciences, and is less precise in its application. Moreover the unity of the system of scientific and research libraries also demands the creation of a unified and centralised reference and bibliographic network, guaranteeing more effective assistance to science and industry.

The republic libraries cooperate in the work of scientific and research libraries by creating a coordinated system of reference and bibliographic service, and by creating reference and bibliographic tools to assist in the organisation and use of their own stocks. Finally, major new tasks now arise in the completion of which the republic libraries play their part. These concern the stock-taking of reference stocks, card indexes and other sources of information located in information agencies and libraries, and active assistance in the mutual use of this reference and coordinating service.

The state of development in the formation of a centralised Union wide reference and bibliographic service is irregular. In the field of cooperation in bibliographical work and the creation of reference and bibliographic guides to stocks, considerable experience has been gained by the republic libraries. The practical realisation of a reference service, including the information and bibliographic stocks of other libraries in the republic, must develop through a number of intermediate stages, which increase the importance of the role played by the republic libraries in information service to science and industry.

MECHANISATION OF LIBRARY AND BIBLIOGRAPHIC PROCESSES

The development of the information work in the republic libraries is related to the mechanisation of library and bibliographic processes. However at the present this problem is being solved extremely slowly. In the libraries, especially in those which have been recently situated in new buildings, some means of mechanisation are used, mainly internal library transport (*eg,* lifts), means of interlibrary links (teletypes) and the photographic reproduction of printed material.

It is urgently necessary to develop a broad long term program (about ten to twelve years) for republic libraries to master new technical resources providing for the complex mechanisation of library and bibliographic processes. To achieve this program demands the development of experimental work in different directions, primarily in the field of bibliographic scanning. It is also necessary to attract specialised constructional organisations to this work, to take into account the economics of the various methods and to obtain staff capable of operating complex technical and retrieval systems.

The question of the formation of special structural subdivisions in the libraries is urgent, especially the establishment of divisions for the mechanisation of library and bibliographic processes as is done, for example, in the state library of the Lithuanian SSR. Such divisions not only should press for means of mechanisation in their libraries, but they should also exert an influence on the practice of other libraries in the republic.

The development of republic libraries as information centres involves the extension of the scientific basis of their work. Many problems in modern conditions cannot be solved speculatively and require scientific investigation, experimental checking, and an examination of the effectiveness.

In this connection, the experiment of state libraries (Ukrainian, Belorussian, Estonian, Moldavian, Latvian, Kirghiz and several other Union republics), which in 1966 were included in a major sociological investigation of professional readers' interests and the inquiries of scientists and specialists (under the direction of the Saltykov-Shchedrin state library), deserves all the approval possible. Even the most provisional analysis of the resultant material shows the fundamental nature of this work, as a result of which important conclusions will be drawn on ways of modernising the information work of republic libraries and the most effective and rational forms and methods of library and bibliographical service to science and industry will be chosen and scientifically based.

REPUBLIC LIBRARIES AS SCIENTIFIC SYSTEM CENTRES

In the early days of the formation of republic libraries under the Soviet administration, they developed as central library institutions, actively influencing the progress and development of all library work in each Union republic. Comprehensive systematic assistance to libraries in the republic, especially to public libraries, which are concerned with book provision and guidance to readers, is included in their functions. This is one of the essential characteristics of the republic libraries, determining to a large extent their socialist nature and their leading role in the development of library affairs in the country.

The system of methodological assistance in its present form given to libraries of the Union republics was built up gradually. The most typical example of this complex process is that the republic libraries (possible to a greater extent than other central libraries) have passed on from ' good advice ', through an analysis of ways of improving library affairs, to the development of scientifically based recommendations and active work in organisation and methods based on general principles. They have been concerned with conclusions drawn from experience gained in the provision of books to the nation and in practical assistance for cultural organisations in the solution of the urgent problems of library development in the republic. The experience of republic libraries has clearly confirmed the position of Soviet library science, considering the scientific and systematic work of the central library as a form of guidance in library affairs.

The completion of the important tasks, for example providing a book service to the broad mass of the people, and systematic unification of the comprehensive work of the libraries, is inconceivable without a firm scientific basis in the development of library affairs. The republic libraries emerge, not only as system centres, but also as the leading institutions for scientific research in library affairs in the republic, solving the most important problems of library science, bibliography and the history of books. The study of the national characteristics of library affairs and bibliographies of national literature has the greatest importance. This side of their activities is a serious contribution to the development of Soviet library science and bibliography, and to the formation of a scientific basis for book promotion and library development in the conditions of such a multinational country as the Soviet Union.[18]

Within the sphere of influence of each of the republic libraries as scientific and systematic centres, there are a considerable number of libraries of different types and forms, belonging to various departments and organisations. For instance, in 1966, systematic assistance was received by ten thousand libraries in the Kazakh SSR, about eight thousand in the Georgian SSR, more than six thousand in the Azerbaijan SSR, more than two thousand in the Turkmen SSR and about 1·3 thousand in the Kirghiz SSR. Among these libraries are public, regional, country, children's, school and special technical libraries. Even this selective data shows how complex are the tasks and how great the scale of the work of republic libraries as methods centres, and also to what degree the forms of systematic guidance which they must employ for the libraries are flexible and adaptable.

In the practice of the republic libraries, the following basic trends in their activities as scientific and systematic centres can be defined:

32

systematic guidance to the state network of public libraries in the Union republics; comprehensive systematic help to all other libraries in the republic, irrespective of the department to which they belong; and coordination of the work of specialised library systems centres, which must be the final aim of a unified system of systematic guidance.

The all-Union value of the experience gained by republic libraries is solving many of the problems encountered in library development, and constitutes the subject matter of their scientific and systematic work. Thus during the post war years, the activities of republic libraries have been directed to the solution of the following problems:

1 An increase in the ideological and theoretical level of the work of libraries and active guidance to readers in order to attract the main body of the people to the use of books. The role of libraries in forming reading circles of different groups in the community and in developing work in accordance with the studies of the interests and inquiries of readers has gradually increased. The republic libraries in particular use more active methods for the promotion of books. More and more use is being made of bibliographies for recommending books.

2 The widest use of library stocks, which is one of the most urgent problems of library development. Its solution is associated with practical assistance by libraries in the more rational and planned acquisition of stocks and with the organisation for promoting new books by all modern means (print, radio, television, cinema, exhibitions and reviews).

3 Practical realisation of a unified system of library service to the people. In recent years, republic libraries have done much in setting up the library network in towns and in the country, the organisation of library service to different groups of the population, especially to children, young people, workers and collective farmers, economists and teachers. Very long term experiments and practical work in the field of centralisation of service to the people by libraries on urban, regional and village soviet scales have been carried out. The contribution of republic libraries to coordination and cooperation in the work of libraries of different departments and organisations in the republic is no less considerable. Some republic

libraries have even introduced the post of chief librarian for co-ordinating the work of libraries of the republic.

4 Rational organisation of the activity of the libraries in accordance with modern requirements, standardisation of the work of libraries in the republic, improved methods of service to readers, rationalisation of library and bibliographic processes and their mechanisation, scientific organisation of the duties of library staff and the constant increase in their professional skill.

During many years of practice in republic libraries, active and effective forms of systematic guidance by libraries were developed and introduced. The searches for these forms of service were not isolated, but were by means of close cooperation between all the republic libraries and working contacts with the Lenin State Library. It is characteristic that in recent years, such forms of systematic guidance, which guarantee an increase in the organisational role of systematic guidance centres of the Union republics and also the more active introduction of the best methods of book service to the people have become widely available. This can be shown by the following examples. Instructional and systematic notes, containing fundamental and precise recommendations on the introduction of progressive experiments in the work of libraries and the organisation of a library service to the people, are very effective. The calling of republic working conferences for library staffs—an active form of collective work on the generalisation of the experience gained in libraries, and the development of recommendations—became a well respected tradition.[19] In all the Union republics much attention was paid to the jubilee working conference, devoted to the whole of the development of library affairs during the fifty years of Soviet rule. Some republic libraries set up experiments which helped to choose the most effective forms and methods of book service to the people (for example, experiments in the branch system).

Republic libraries now participate more actively in the work of the Ministries of Culture of the Union republics in the preparation of decrees, instructions, provisions and other standard documents on library affairs. Thus in 1966 to 1967, on the basis of an all-Union report[20] and general conclusions from the experience of the republics, regulations were prepared, with the participation of the republic libraries, concerning the organisation of the network of libraries, which took into account the national features of library affairs, the present conditions, the types of populated areas, and the density of population.

The republic libraries provided a vital influence in the establishment and development of a central system of systematic guidance to libraries. It was constructed in conformity with the administrative and territorial divisions of the Union republics. In comparatively small republics, the republic library renders immediate assistance also to central and district libraries. In these cases, the scientific and systematic work is as closely related as possible to the precise problems of library institutions in the town and country. In the large Union republics, having regional administrative and territorial divisions, a more complex scheme for organising the systematic guidance by libraries is employed, and republic libraries mainly concentrate their efforts on the development of regional links in the system of methodical guidance and their effects on the library network of the republic through the regional libraries.

An experiment in the organisation of systematic work to assist the libraries in the Ukrainian SSR is of interest. In the republic there are twenty six regions with highly developed industries and agriculture. In 1966, the branched state library network of the Ukraine included five large science libraries, forty nine regional (including twenty five children's) libraries, 788 district (including children's) libraries and more than 14 thousand rural and other libraries, which presented very complex problems for the organisation of systematic guidance to libraries. Based on the republic library of the Ukraine and three great general science libraries (in Kharkov, Odessa and L'vov), zonal systematic centres were formed, each of which guides libraries within a group of regions, and also works out various problems and generalises experience in book promotion, and guidance to readers in specific subject areas for all the libraries of the republic.[21]

A coordinated system of methodological guidance has been developed with the participation of each Union library. Joint planning (long term and day to day) of the scientific systematic work of the central libraries must be directed towards the most easily attained practical solution of the problem. Similar plans are compiled on the initiative of the republic libraries everywhere and play a considerable role in unifying the efforts of the scientific systematic centres.

The task undertaken is considerable. The republic libraries now face new perspectives associated with the wider use of their rich book stocks. The interests of scientific and technical progress and the further development of the productive forces of the country and the whole practice of communist development demands the utter efficiency in the activities of the state libraries of the Union republics.

LITERATURE REFERENCES AND NOTES

1 *Gosudarstvennaya biblioteka Latviiskoi SSR imeni Vilisa Latsisa* (Vilis Latis State Library of the Latvian SSR), page 9. Riga, Putevoditel, 1966.

2 *Gosudartstennaya respublikanskaya publichnaya biblioteka Gruzinskoi SSR imeni K Marksa* (K Marx State Republic Library of the Georgian SSR), page 8. Tiflis, 1963.

3 *Azerbaidzhanskaya republikanskaya biblioteka imeni M F Akhundova* (M F Akhundov Library of the Azerbaijan Republic), Baku, 1963.

4 R O Talman: *Gosudarstvennaya publichnaya biblioteka Tadzhikskoi SSR imeni Firdousi* (Firdousa State Public Library of the Tadzhik SSR), Stalinbad, 1954.

5 All the statistical data included in the paper without indication of source are taken from the reports of the republic libraries 1959-1965.

6 Outline of the history of the Communist Party State Library of the Ukrainian SSR, in *Skarbnitsya lyuds'kogo rozumu* (Treasure house of human knowledge), Kharkov, State Republic Library of the Ukrainian SSR, 1966.

7 Before this, manuals and regulations concerning the separate libraries were in operation, devised and adopted at various times by republic cultural organisations. The *Exemplary manual* standardised the designation of republic libraries to *State library of the … Soviet Socialist Republic.*

8 For example, *see* V P Lirov: (National bibliography and patriotic bibliography) *Sovetskaya bibliografiya,* 67 (3) 1961, pages 41-50; V P Lirov: (Problems of a national bibliography in the light of the Leninist principle) *Sovetskaya bibliografiya,* 90 (2) 1965, pages 13-26.

9 For more details about these principles, *see* I V Gudovshchikova: (On the concept of the 'National bibliography') *Sovetskaya bibliografiya,* 57 (5) 1959, pages 78-88; G P Fonotov: (Problems of a general retrospective bibliography in the national republics) *Sovetskaya bibliografiya,* 94 (6) 1965, pages 3-13; I V Gudovshchikova: ('Patriotic' bibliography, national and territorial bibliography) *Sovetskaya bibliografiya,* 100 (6) 1966, pages 23-42.

10 For the subjects of the conference and the propositions made, *see Sovetskaya bibliografiya,* 94 (6) 1965, pages 3-13, 88-93; 95 (1) 1966, pages 3-63; 96 (2) 1966, pages 42-59.

11 For example, *see: Periodicheskie izdaniya UkrSSR* (Periodical publications of the Ukrainian SSR) 1918-1950, Zhurnaly (Journals) (in Ukrainian), Kharkov, UkrSSR Book Chamber, 1956: *Periodicheskaya pechat Belorussii 1817-1916* (Bibliographic index, periodical publications of Belorussia 1817-1916), Minsk, Belorussian SSR Book Chamber, 1960.

12 For example, *see: Uzbekistan, bibliog. ukazatel lit.* (Uzbekistan, bibliographic index of the literature) 4 vols, Tashkent, Nava State Public Library of the Uzbek SSR, 1960-1962. *Latviiskaya SSR, 1940-1960, ukazetel lit.* (Latvian SSR, 1940-1960, index to the literature), Riga, State Library of the Latvian SSR, 1961.

13 This problem came to light in a paper with a number of propositions with which, however, it is impossible to agree: A N Buchenkov: (Folklore in a scheme of library and bibliographic work in the Union republics) in *Trudy* (Proceedings) Lenin State Library USSR, 7 1963, pages 80-92.

14 For example, *see* S B Tomonis: (Some problems of bibliography for the recommendation of books in the Union republics) *Sovetskaya bibliografiya,* 98 (4) 1966 pages 3-12; M Kheiman: (The development of bibliography for the recommended books in the Estonian SSR), in *Nauchnaya konferentsiya bibliotechnykh rabotnikov, posvyashennaya 20-letnei godovshchine Estonskoi SSR*

37

(Scientific conference of library workers with 20 years' experience in the Estonian SSR) Tallin, 1961 (in Estonian).

15 *Sobranie postanovlenii pravitel'stva SSSR* (Collected government resolutions of the USSR) (25) page 220. Moscow, 1966.

16 (Scientific information service) *Pravda,* 12 January 1967.

17 The State bibliographic registration of printed works, organised in all the Union republics and successfully carried out by the republic book chambers is one of the greatest achievements of Soviet national bibliography. For example, *see* A Yazberdiev: (The Book Chamber of the Turkmen SSR and its bibliographic activity) *Sovetskaya bibliografiya,* 98 (4) 1966, pages 24-31.

18 In recent years in the Union republics, a number of well considered reviews on the bibliography and history of library matters have appeared. For example, *see* I B Simanovskii: *Belorusskaya sovetskaya bibliografiya* (Belorussian Soviet bibliography) part 1. Minsk, State Library of the Belorussian SSR and Book Chamber of the Belorussian SSR, 1965.

19 Scientific practice conferences were arranged in almost all the Union republics during 1965-1967. *See: Biblioteki SSSR, Opyt raboty,* 31 1966, pages 155-156, 159-162; 32 1966, pages 153-155; 33 1967, pages 156-157; 34 1967, pages 159-161.

20 (Exemplary regulations for the organisation of a unified network of public libraries), *Bibliotekar,* (1) 1967, pages 54-56.

21 For more details on this, *see* Z A Pechenezhskaya and I V Shazhko: (Some problems of organisational and systematic guidance to the libraries of the Ukraine) *Biblioteki SSSR, Opyt raboty,* 30 1965, pages 93-103; I M Kirillov: (Experience in the organisational and systematic guidance to libraries in the area) *Biblioteki SSSR, opyt raboty,* 33 1966, pages 104-114.

III SOVIET PUBLIC LIBRARIES

by E A FENELONOV

One of the most basic indications of the library situation within a country is the level to which the public libraries have developed. It is therefore important to consider the evolution of the public library system, providing as it does such an essential contribution to the culture and education of the people, since the inception of Soviet administration fifty years ago.

The young Soviet state inherited a very sparse library system. For example in the whole of Russia, in 1913, there were about 14 thousand libraries with a book stock of 9·4 million volumes. The money spent annually on the contents of these libraries, according to the estimates of B B Veselovskii, totalled approximately 5 million roubles. In order to show how much this sum is, it is recalled that the price of one book at this time was fifty kopeks.[1] Money was allotted by the elective district councils, enlightened societies and private subscribers. The state exchequer did not supply library grants. It was not surprising that libraries, being set up for the people, eked out a miserable existence and for years did not obtain any new bookstocks. Three quarters of the libraries, answering a questionnaire from the Society of Library Science in 1911, had in their stock less than a thousand books, about a quarter of them from 1902 to 1910 being unable to buy a single book.[2] It was reckoned that a library enjoyed good conditions if it was accommodated in one not very large room in a school, school corridor or cloakroom. An established librarian was a rarity and specialised library equipment did not exist.

Summing up the fifty years of activity, from 1856, in the organisation of adult education including also library matters, the elective district councils recognised that the expenditure on these activities was insufficient to satisfy the elementary cultural necessities of the population.[3]

Since libraries for the people were administered by voluntary bodies it is impossible to make specific statements about their instructive activities. However thousands of cases are known of the closing of libraries, withdrawal from stock of books which were

39

objectionable to the tsarist administration, and the legal persecution of librarians.

After the victory of the great October Socialist Revolution, the basic pattern of public library activities changed. The Communist Party always saw in libraries one of the most important institutions contributing to the development of culture for the people, and considered an adjustment in the work of libraries a necessary condition for the construction of socialism. Even during the first years of the new administration special attention was paid to the development of library affairs.

Libraries had to promote the propaganda of communist ideology, as well as giving the people a certain amount of scientific knowledge on nature and society and to make readily available basic polytechnic education. It was demanded from libraries, as from other ideological establishments, that they should ' educate the public strictly towards a revolutionary outlook and revolutionary action '.[4]

The new tasks for libraries dictated the necessity for the introduction of serious changes in the organisation of the public library service. They were faced with the restoration of existing book stocks of the people's libraries, and it made sense to replace them at the expense of commandeered volumes and entire private collections, as well as with newly published literature. Following this, thousands of libraries were opened, accommodation and equipment were provided, personnel devoted to affairs of the revolution were selected, trained and directed in library work.

It is well known that even during these first years of Soviet rule, some party and government resolutions and decrees on library affairs were taken and that in spite of an extraordinary pressure of work, Lenin personally concerned himself with these problems.

By the decree of the Council of People's Commissars ' on the protection of libraries and storehouses for books ' laid down by Lenin in July 1918, all book collections (public, private, and district council) were acknowledged as the property of the general public. The People's Commissariat of Education was instructed to take swift and comprehensive steps to assign these book resources to the whole population so as to create a wide library network capable of providing books in even the remotest corners of Russia.

Accomplishing this directive, in the difficult conditions of civil war, the members of the Soviet government, with the constant support and assistance of party organisations, founded the basis of a planned library system.

Much attention was turned to establishing a network of library points, permitting the use of the very modest material and book resources by the largest possible number of readers. In addition to the permanent libraries, thousands of cottage reading rooms and travelling libraries were created. Moreover democratic principles were applied to the organisation of the library network. We should mention that in pre-revolutionary Russia, the tsarist administration, forced to give permission for the opening of national libraries, urgently recommended the creation of large libraries, which were used by a limited circle of people.

In 1920, soon after the Revolution, the state of library affairs in the country was assessed. A survey indicated that the number of permanent libraries in Russia, in comparison with the last five years of the pre-revolutionary period, had increased by 100 percent in provinces, where, in the pre-revolutionary period, the library network had been considered sufficient, and by three to five hundred percent in provinces where libraries had been scarce.[5] With the introduction of new economic policies, rapid growth of the library network was somewhat slowed, and because of the difficult economic position of the government, the grant for library construction was reduced. But by 1925, as soon as the period of reconstruction ended, steady growth in the number of public libraries again took place.

As a significant yardstick determining the beginning of the new stage in library construction, we have the 1925 resolution of the Central Committee of the Russian Communist Party of Bolsheviks ' On village libraries and popular literature for stock of libraries '.[6] From this time, the expansion and modernisation of the public library system proceeded at a more rapid rate. Over the five year period (1925-1930), the number of public libraries in the country as a whole increased one and a half times and the book stock almost twice (*cf* diagram).

The permanent libraries were strengthened and their number increased, especially in the small rural districts and regional centres. These libraries were considered as bases, organising all the library work for territories, rural districts and regions.

41

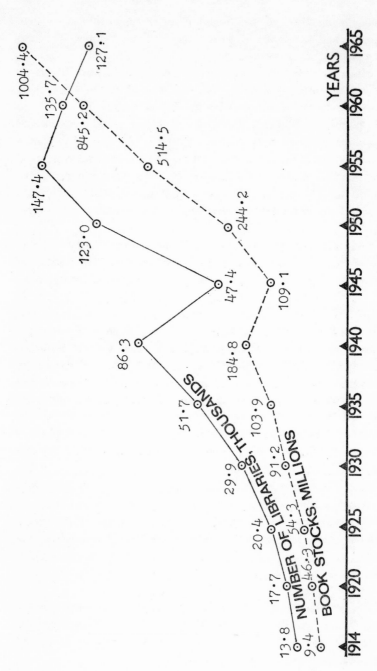

Growth of public libraries and their book stocks

Between 1930 and 1935 the number of public libraries doubled, their stock markedly increased and the quality of book collections improved. An ever increasing interest in the growth of these libraries was taken by the trade unions and social cooperative organisations. In the thirties the network of research, student and technical libraries also vigorously increased. In connection with this, it became necessary to define more accurately the range of problems with which the public library must be engaged in the general library system, and to determine the principles in the organisation of the network and the basic coordination of the work of libraries of different types.

In the thirties N K Krupskaia made a great contribution to the development of public libraries, in particular to their educational and training functions, and to improvements in cooperation between libraries of various types and belonging to different departments.

N Konstantinovna assessed the work of the public library first of all from the viewpoint that it provided for the public material which assisted in the solution of the political and economic problems facing the Socialist State. ' The difference between the Soviet library and other libraries rests in the fact that our Soviet library must stand far closer to the public, be more closely connected with the public, and the public must consider library matters as its vital concern.'[7]

In the last five years before the war the number of libraries increased from 51·7 thousand to 86·3 thousand and the book stock from 103·9 million copies to 184·8 million.

The fascist invasion caused great damage to the public library system. Only in 1949-1950 was it restored to the pre-war conditions. From 1950 to 1955, the quantitative growth of permanent libraries, mobile libraries, branch libraries and distribution points continued. New tendencies appeared in the development of the system—namely the process of gradual change from simple to more modern sophisticated forms of service. The strengthening of the small library institutions also continued. The club library, having a small book stock and without a librarian ceased to satisfy readers' inquiries. Beginning in 1953, club libraries were largely replaced by rural libraries and the former became branch libraries. In 1952 it was reckoned that there were more than 57 thousand club libraries and in five years their number was reduced to 30 thousand. At the present time there are no more than 5 to 7 thousand libraries of this type operating.

A similar process also affected the collective libraries. So long as the state remained uninterested in the possibilities of developing rural libraries, the collective libraries were a great help in the provision of books for the rural population. In view of the growth in the number of independent rural libraries, collective libraries in many places closed and their book stocks were transferred to the state libraries. The number of collective libraries now amounts to 5 thousand (in 1950 there were 22 thousand and in 1960 there were 9 thousand).

In recent years the collectives very frequently assigned considerable resources to the upkeep of state libraries. For instance in one Krasnodar region, the resources of the collectives provided more than 100 rural library staff and about 100 thousand roubles were provided annually for bookstocks. When in 1965, in the rural parts of Russia, a reorganisation of the library system from collectives into rural libraries took place, a further 2 million roubles were forthcoming for the acquisition of books and equipment. In operation today in towns and rural areas are more than 127 thousand independent public libraries, 220 thousand mobile and almost 9 thousand branch libraries.

With the unprecedented earlier growth of book stocks in the post-war period, some reduction in the actual number of public libraries did not lessen the progressive increase in stock to any great extent. In 1965, in public library book collections, there were more than 1,000 million volumes. The majority of public libraries have on average 6,000 volumes and a fifth have 10,000 volumes. Public library stocks include literature which enable a large number of readers' inquiries to be satisfied.

As a result of the years of Soviet rule, the conditions for library activities have radically changed. After the revolution, the best of the requisitioned premises were diverted for libraries both in town and villages. In the thirties, as soon as the economic position permitted, special library buildings were constructed. According to data from the all-Union library census of 1934, of the 16 thousand public libraries, two thirds occupied more than 20 square metres. The average library occupies twice as much area.[8]

Thousands of public libraries are now situated in specially equipped, spacious, bright and comfortable rooms, providing readers appropriate facilities for the selection and reading of literature. About forty percent of all public libraries have rooms larger than 50 square metres and a tenth have more than 150 square metres.

The degree of development in the public library network after fifty years of Soviet rule can be gauged from the following: the number of libraries increased nine times, the size of the book stock increasing 100 times. As regards to the facilities of libraries (area of rooms, equipment, etc) and also the number of qualified members of staff, the level now achieved is in general difficult to compare with the pre-revolution conditions. Every year about 180 million roubles are spent on bookstocks for public libraries, an expenditure which is increasing annually.

The public library service after the revolution was formed primarily as a state system. Of the 127 thousand public libraries in existence now, more than 84-90 thousand are supported by the state library establishment, and it is here that ninety percent of the library stock and the bulk of the qualified librarians are concentrated.

After fifty years of Soviet rule, the strength of the library system in the USSR has increased, it having become comprehensive and having improved its internal organisation. Continuous refinement of services led to the formation of several varieties of public libraries. Thus in the thirties, a network of independent children's libraries in towns and villages took shape. Such libraries, merely systems of the Ministry of Culture, now amount to nearly 5 thousand with a total book stock of about 70 million volumes.

The differentiation of libraries according to their service to readers of different age groups of the population continues today, and proof of this is the creation of independent youth libraries. In Russia there are about twenty five of these. There were also great changes in the organisational structure of the library system and a precise grading of public libraries was instituted.

The activities of smaller library institutions belonging to various departments coincide at various stages with central libraries. At the same time, the central libraries satisfy readers' inquiries of a more advanced type. At present, central urban and reference libraries operate in towns, and libraries of regional centres and libraries of administrative centres of the village soviets (central rural) operate in the country. In the public library system there are reckoned to be about 2 thousand central urban, several thousand reference libraries, and 3,935 regional libraries, as well as 1,200 regional children's libraries. There are at least 10,000 central/rural libraries in the country.

The present organisation of the public library network permits on the one hand, differentiation in services, and on the other the amalgamation of all public libraries into one system, guaranteeing effective flow of books to the public with the least expenditure of state and public funds. It is important to mention that libraries in our country work in close cooperation with libraries of other types and are part of the whole state library system.

The system of public library service created during the years of Soviet rule immeasurably expanded its potential with the use of books from public funds. Fifty years ago libraries were located near the homes of the majority of the readers in only a few provinces. For example, three quarters of the territory of the whole of the Russian empire was devoid of libraries. Today almost eighty percent of town residents, workmen's settlements and villages have libraries or their branches within fifteen to twenty minutes walk. Part of the remaining twenty percent of the inhabitants can borrow books from their place of work, which also does not involve a great expenditure of time.

It is also important to note that the majority of public libraries are open for not less than forty six hours per week at times suitable for the public, while in the USA, for example, half the libraries serve readers less than twenty four hours in a week.[9] These facts again emphasise the accessibility of Soviet public libraries.

In recent years, the number of readers has increased annually by 2 to 3 million. State public libraries alone serve about 63 million or twenty seven percent of the population. In a number of regions, *eg* Kalinin and Yaroslav, libraries actually supply books to the whole adult population and to all students. On an average throughout the country, each reader borrows more than twenty books a year, and of these roughly six are concerned with social politics, natural science and industry.

The role of the librarian in carrying out library service in our country involves not only the distribution of books and information about available literature at the request of a reader, but assistance in the formation of a true ideological attitude in the reader, the growth of his professional craftsmanship, an increase in general culture and at the same time that the individual may actively and consciously take part in socialist construction.

Data concerning measures to popularise books are, to a certain extent, characteristic of the range of the ideological and educational work of the public libraries of the USSR. In 1965, in individual state public libraries alone, almost 4 million such efforts were made in which not less than 60 million readers took part. A third of these measures had as their object the provision of help to industry. Public libraries organise more than 2 million book exhibitions and have 10 million individual discussions and consultations each year.

Careful examination of the interests of specific groups and categories of readers, constant observation of the formation of tastes and tendencies in literature, today permit the provision on a scientific basis of guidance in reading to thousands of people using public libraries.

This enormous work is carried out in the interests of all classes. Public libraries in the USSR are today libraries of the people, working in the very midst of the people and for them. More than 1·5 million people are active workers in libraries, 500 thousand take part in activities of library soviets. An annual report on the work of the library carried out for the people is a form of national control.

During the past fifty years, enormous advances have been made in the organisation of public library service to the people and undoubtedly further increases will be made in the next few years.[10] Great attention must be paid to perfecting schemes for promoting books on all subjects and to the formation of reading circles for various strata of society on the basis of a careful examination of their interests. Library practice must not be developed without giving the closest consideration to sociology, without investigating the problem of free time for specific categories of readers, and the factors determining their demand for books. It is to be hoped that the investigation into the interests of readers of different categories,[11] organised by the V I Lenin State Library of the USSR in 1963 to 1967, will help in forming important conclusions for the improvement of the whole system of assistance in the choice of books by public libraries.

In the furtherance of self education the working public library as usual preserves its leading importance. But in order for it to fulfil its function at a level corresponding to the modern requirements of readers, we are faced with hard work and the solution of a number of organisational problems. One of these consists of clear demarcation of the functions of public and special libraries. Without discriminating between the duties of these libraries we cannot eliminate duplication of services and can not achieve rapid increases in the quality of work with readers, for the most effective use of book collections. In relation to this, problems concerning the optimal size and composition of the stocks for different kinds of public libraries and their form of work with readers will be solved.

Almost complete satisfaction of the library requirements of the inhabitants is outlined in the five year plan of development for the library system. At present promising work in the organisation of the library network has developed almost everywhere, and the search for more effective forms of organisation of services has been conducted. A system of organisational and methodical guidance for libraries is also being perfected.

The work which has been done recently by cultural bodies and trade unions, to organise the library network in towns, is a very important step in the increasing effectiveness of library services. As a result considerable economies in material resources have been achieved as duplication was eliminated in the arrangement of libraries, in the acquisition of stocks and in service to readers. A united system of organisational and systematic guidance for libraries has been created.

The results accomplished by the cultural units, the crux of which led to the transformation of one of the libraries into a central library institution and the rest into its branches[12] are very encouraging. Affiliation provided for complete unification of the stock, the staff and the resources, and therefore as far as possible, conformity with libraries of the same category.

The considerable advances achieved after the years of Soviet rule in library construction hold the promise of the further growth in the effectiveness of the public library system. We are now approaching the time when, with the help of experts in public and other libraries, every citizen in our country will be able to obtain regular and rapid answer to any problem.

LITERATURE REFERENCES AND NOTES

1 B B Veselovskii: (The problem of the development of a normal network of rural libraries for readers) *Zemskoe delo* (11-12) 1911, pages 847-859.

2 K N Rubinskii: (The position of library affairs in Russia and other states) *Trudy pervogo vserossiiskogo s'ezda po bibilotechnomu delu* (Proceedings of the first All Russian Congress on library affairs) (2) page 11. St Petersburg 1912.

3 V I Charnoluskii: (The Elective District Council and out-of-school education) *Yubileinyi zemskii sbornik* (Collected papers Jubilee Elective District Council), pages 388-390. St Petersburg 1914.

4 V I Lenin: Complete collected works Vol 44, page 422. Moscow.

5 E N Medynskii: *Vneshkol'noe obrazovanie v RSFSR. Statisticheskii obzor* (Out-of-school education in the RSFSR. A statistical review), second edition, page 49. Moscow 1923.

6 *Materialy k istorii bibliotechnogo dela v SSSR* (Material relevant to the history of library affairs in the USSR) 1917-1959, pages 80-83. Leningrad 1960.

7 N K Krupskaia: *O bibliotechnom dele, sbornik* (Library affairs, collected papers), page 91. Moscow 1957.

8 *Vsesoyuznaya bibliotechnaya perepis* (all-Union library census) 1934, Vol 2, pages 232-233. Moscow 1936.

9 *Bibliotechnoe delo v zarubezhnykh stranakh* (Library affairs in foreign countries), page 201. Moscow, Kniga 1965.

10 V Serov, A Malakhov and E Fenelonov: ' Persektivy biblio-technogo stroitel'stva v RSFSR ' (Prospects in library structure in the RSFSR) *Bibliotekar* (1) 1967, pages 1-9.

11 *Chitatel'skie interesy rabochei molodezhi* (Reading interests of young workers) Moscow, Kniga 1966; *Kollektivom sotrydnikov Gosudarstvennoi biblioteki SSSR imeni V I Lenin v 1967 podgo-tovlen dlya pechati sbornik statei—Sovetskii chitatel* (The collected papers, *The Soviet reader,* was prepared for printing by the staff of the V I Lenin State Library of the USSR in 1967).

12 R Z Zotova: (Problems of library service for inhabitants of towns) *Biblioteki SSSR, 34,* 1967, pages 85-99; I Belen'kii : (They are not isolated but in one system. The organisation of an experiment with partial centralisation of the library service) *Biblio-tekar* (3), 1967, pages 3-7; I Ivaneev: (The experiment justifies itself) *Bibliotekar* (3), 1967, pages 7-9.

IV TECHNICAL LIBRARIES IN THE USSR
by T F KARATYGINA

Technical libraries in the USSR are entirely the offspring of the Great October Revolution; they are a new type of library institution. Their creation and development resulted from a socialistic industrialised country requiring the most intensive and planned use of science, from the formation of a great number of scientific and technical institutions serving industry and utilising the newest techniques from both our own and foreign countries, and from the unprecedented growth in the publication of technical literature.

The basis of construction of the technical library network, as in all systems of Soviet libraries, incorporated the Leninist principles of planned organisation and centralisation of library affairs, rational distribution of literature and active use of stocks. The most important tasks for Soviet technical libraries are participation in ideological and educational work, with the object of mobilising the people in the struggle for the creation of a material and technical basis for communism, the forming of a communistic outlook and education, providing information on the most recent scientific and technical literature in the main areas of technical interest in the USSR, giving active help in the solution of precise industrial problems, use of the achievements of technology and the latest industrial experience, wide promotion of technical information to assist in raising the technical level of workers.

On the eve of the semi-centennial jubilee of the October Revolution, technical libraries represent one of the most powerful and well established library networks. About 20 thousand technical libraries were counted in the Soviet Union at the beginning of 1967, functioning at works, factories, mines, building projects and in scientific research, design and constructional organisations attached to departmental committees and ministries, under planning committees of the Soviet republics and central technical information bureaux. The technical libraries possess valuable stocks of journals, books and other technical literature (in all almost 300 million items) and serve 10 million workers in science and industry.

In pre-revolutionary Russia technical libraries were an extremely

51

rare phenomena. According to somewhat inaccurate data, out of the total of fifty six libraries, twenty one were in works and factories, twenty two were attached to technical societies and committees, five were scientific and technical libraries of government institutions and private industrial concerns, and seven were scientific and technical libraries of research institutions and laboratories.[1] Moreover, such a library had to be called a ' polytechnical museum '.

Works and factory libraries were accessible only to a chosen circle of engineering and technical workers and administrators. Thus only four men were admitted to the library of Count Shuvalov, the owner of the Lys'venskii iron foundry—the managers of the area and of the works and two of their assistants, thus strictly preserving industrial secrets. The factory regulations of the Guzhon works (now the Hammer and Sickle works) prohibited the workers from using the library. Many such examples can be cited.

Pre-revolutionary technical libraries were often indebted for their origin to senior scientific/technical workers and primarily to scientific/technical societies and committees. Among the founders and active propagandists for libraries were the revolutionary A L Linev, G M Krzhizhanovskii, the founder of Russian aviation, N E Zhubkovskii and others. The library of the Society of Electrical Engineers was of special importance. On its initiative, an examination of the demand for technical books by workers was organised in 1912, and attempts were undertaken to issue popular literature on applied science (numerous papers in *Byulletenyzkh obshchestva elektrotekhnikov*—Bulletins of the Society of Electrical Engineers) in 1912-1916 serve to confirm this.[2] In 1913 the advisability of the creation of a general technical library, serving many branches of industry, was first discussed here,[3] only finding practical realisation in 1918.

During the Soviet period, the number of the technical libraries rapidly increased, forming an interconnected network with radically changed functions. The tasks of the Soviet technical library were determined by its role in technical progress and the industrial technical education of workers, the raising of the qualifications of engineering staff and the dissemination of information on advanced experimental work. It has become an integral part of industrial undertakings, scientific research institutes and construction bureaux, and has confirmed the technical library as a specific type of library with a specific field of work and organisation.

Into the technical libraries after the October Revolution, beside scholars and engineering workers, there came new readers and workers to whom Soviet rule opened the way to creative work and knowledge.

The technical libraries of the world's first socialist state have a number of fundamental differences in comparison with libraries in the capitalist countries. The purpose of the technical library in the USSR is to make science and technology accessible to the wide masses of the population. In bourgeois states, the popularising of books to help to raise the cultural and technical level of workers does not enter into the duties of the technical libraries. The methods of work applied by technical libraries and the structure of the network of capitalist countries is explained to a large extent by the narrowness of the reader orientation. Technical libraries are limited to reference, bibliographic and information service for business circles.

In contrast to the Soviet Union (where it is scarcely possible to name any large industrial undertaking, scientific institution, ministry, committee or department without a library), the technical libraries of capitalist countries do not cover all the stages of industrial production; they are only attached to the leading industrial institutions, mostly in industrial and commercial companies, firms or laboratories. D Bedsole, making a survey of libraries of 117 corporations in the USA, separated the following principal types: 1) a single central library of a corporation; 2) a central library with a network of branches; 3) an independent library, serving a branch of industry. As a rule they are closed to outsiders and apart from co-workers in the firm, only occasionally serve regular customers and firms connected with them.[4]

The great disparity between the organisation and administration of the work of technical libraries in the USSR and in bourgeois states is emphasised more than once by foreign library scientists. For example, Eva Winter, the librarian of the scientific library of a paper company in Venezuela, pointing out that 'communists more than anyone look after the spreading of libraries' drew the conclusion that 'the difference in the system of Soviet libraries and information services from the library and technical information services in the West consists in their ideological direction on the one hand and in their structure on the other'.[5] The social and economic relationships on the one hand create all the conditions for wide dissemination of scientific and technical experience and the technical enlightenment of workers, and on the other prevent this in practice.

The basic features of the Soviet technical libraries were formulated during the course of development of the Soviet State and socialist industries.[6] In 1917 to 1918, libraries were established in industrial undertakings, followed by libraries of central organisations directing industry and of importance in many fields (Supreme Council of National Economy, its central board and divisions), libraries of scientific research institutes, industrial combines and economic organisations, and educational libraries (technical colleges and technical schools). Thus at the end of 1917, the library of the 'Elektrik' works in Leningrad was created, and in 1919 the library of the 'Red Triangle' (Leningrad), the Tula small arms factory, the Podol mechanical works and others. During these same years the largest libraries of branches of industry appeared: from 1918, the library of the People's Commissariat of Means of Communication began functioning, as did the central library of the petroleum industry from 1919, and the library of the building industry from 1923.

Industrialisation of national economy, the struggle to equip industrial undertakings with new techniques, and the introduction of up to date technology demanded the creation of a library serving many branches of the industrial system, the stocks of which would be fully representative of the literature reflecting the latest experience gained in this country and abroad. It must effectively serve all undertakings and institutions of the Supreme Council of National Economy, assist in the creation of other technical libraries and serve as a systematic base for the libraries of heavy industry. This role was assumed by the State Scientific Library, attached to the Scientific and Technical Managing Board of the Supreme Council of National Economy, and formed in 1927 from the three libraries of the Supreme Council of National Economy: the state scientific, technical and economic library of the Scientific and Technical Division of the Supreme Council of National Economy (1918), the central library of the Praesidium of the Supreme Council of National Economy (1918) and the special reading room for foreign literature attached to the Bureau of Foreign Science and Technology of the Scientific Technical Society of the Supreme Council of National Economy (1920).[7]

From 1928 to 1941 the establishment of a soundly constructed network of technical libraries took place within the USSR. The reconstruction of all branches of the national economy, based on new techniques, the change in management of industry and its direct approach to production, served as a foundation for its formation. The pre-war period differed solely in the rapid growth of the technical libraries in industrial undertakings. A decisive role in their planned creation and development was played by the resolution of the Central Committee of the all-Union Communist Party of 25 March 1931 on ' The organisation of industrial and technical propaganda '.[8]

At the beginning of the thirties systematic guidance to technical libraries was entrusted to the state scientific library. From the moment of creation of a special group (at the end of 1931), the state scientific library began to carry out the function of a methodology centre for the libraries of heavy industry.

In the five years preceding the war, a wide network of technical libraries was formed in various industrial regions of our country, a new type of network being formed, namely that of libraries in training centres. Libraries in scientific research institutes received further development. On account of the increase in the cultural and technical level of the working class, the number of reader/workers using the libraries of their industrial undertakings increased considerably. The first all-Russian conference of workers in technical libraries of the heavy industries (January 1939) was important in determining the basic direction of work in technical libraries during this period.[9]

Differentiation in guidance to industry, expressed by the division of the Supreme Council of National Economy in 1932 into a number of independent councils of people's commissariats (heavy, light, timber and food industries) led to the necessity of forming independent libraries attached to them. The State Scientific Library, transferred to the People's Commissariat of Heavy Industries, was legally designated as a centre of organisational and methodological guidance for libraries of heavy industry as well as a bibliographic centre for technical literature. Increase in the scientific and technical staffs in industry and the rapid development of technical libraries away from the centre demanded the creation of geographic branches of the State Scientific Library, which were simultaneously multi-aspect technical libraries and reference centres for the State Scientific Library, accomplishing organisational and methodological guidance to technical libraries.

In the heavy industry system at the beginning of 1941, technical libraries appeared which were confined to specific forms of literature. These were the Central Library of Structural Plans, the Library of Technical Catalogues and the Library of Standards and Patents.

During the war years technical libraries were reconstructed in accordance with wartime conditions. The necessity for central libraries in the People's Commissariats for industry was realised during this period, and they were set up with special urgency in almost all the People's Commissariats. In connection with the evacuation of industry from the temporarily occupied areas to the Urals and Siberia, the State Scientific Library organised new diversified geographic branches in the east of the country (in Perm, Barnaul and Karagand) which established a service for the evacuated industrial undertakings. After the liberation of Rostov, Stalingrad, Kharkov and Kiev, the state scientific library did much for the restoration of its branches. The total quantity of literature destroyed and removed by German invaders reached 8 million volumes. By the middle forties, sixteen branches of the State Scientific Library were already in existence (four in Moscow and twelve in the provinces). New branches were created in the Donetz Basin and the work of branches in Kiev and Leningrad recommenced. In the second half of the forties, the main task was the restoration of those libraries destroyed by the fascists. Organisational guidance to technical libraries was increased and this is shown in the development of central libraries for the separate People's Commissariats. After the reorganisation of the People's Commissariats into ministries in March 1946, the differentiation of technical libraries into branches of industry continued.

In connection with the transfer in 1946 of the State Scientific Library to the Ministry of Higher Education in accordance with the Government resolution, it was confirmed that the library was empowered to be a diversified technical library. With this it was also given new functions, namely guidance to libraries of higher educational institutes.

In accordance with the resolution of the Twentieth Congress of the Communist Party and the February (1957) plenary meeting of the Central Committee of the Communist Party, the territorial structure of control of the national economy was accepted. The network of technical libraries in administrative and economic regions became the main link in the system of library and bibliographic service to industry.[10] First of all attention was drawn to the creation of libraries in the technological centres in the economic districts based upon branches of the State Scientific Library and to libraries based on individual branches of industry, being the central scientific technical libraries of the former ministries. Duplicate stocks were exchanged between the great libraries of the country and various types of specialised scientific and technical libraries. Central scientific and technical libraries were established, as were republic scientific technical libraries, in the Union republics. They were to serve the workers in industry in the sections of each economic district, and were to form a network of technical libraries within their district to give the workers systematic assistance. The organisation of central scientific technical libraries and regional scientific technical libraries plays a considerable part in the improvement of library and bibliographic service to industrial production and in organisational and methodological guidance to technical libraries.

The majority of the libraries of the Council of National Economy were converted in a comparatively short time into spacious book stores and centres for systematic guidance to the technical libraries of economic districts (for example, the central scientific and technical library of Stavropol and Kuibishev Regional Economic Councils). As distinct from being geographic branches of the State Scientific library, the central technical libraries established closer economic bonds with the organisational bodies of the administrative and

57

economic districts, providing opportunities for satisfying demands for books and bibliographies with maximum efficiency. They also supervised the development of the local technical libraries and became important links in the economic control of the industry of every economic district.

In 1958, a central library covering a large number of branches of Soviet industry, namely the State Public Scientific and Technical Library of the USSR, was created.[11] From the beginning it was developed as a central book store for the many branches of scientific, technical and industrial literature and documentation from our country and abroad. The State Public Scientific and Technical Library gave direct systematic guidance to the scientific and technical libraries of the committees of the Council of Ministers of the Union Republics, ministries and departments, and coordinated the work of all technical and scientific libraries in the country.[12]

Simultaneously the State Scientific Library of the Ministry of Higher Education was transferred to the Siberian division of the Academy of Science of the USSR. The State Public Scientific and Technical Library of the Siberian division of the Academy of Science of the USSR was organised in Novosibirsk, based on the State Scientific Library.

Together with the network of technical libraries organised on a geographic basis, scientific and technical libraries were established for branches of industry connected with departments, committees and ministries. A number of them, for example, the central scientific and technical library of the Ministry of Communication, Sea and Inland-water Transport etc, normally carried out not only library and bibliographic work but also methodological guidance to the libraries in subordinate industrial undertakings and organisations of the ministry. The type of work carried out by other libraries being set up by branches of the state public scientific and technical library of the USSR, substantially changed. They were deprived of their methodological function and ceased to fulfil the role of central libraries organising library and bibliographic service to workers in separate branches of industry. In fact their duties were reduced to serving the engineering and technical staff in Moscow.

During 1962 and 1963 the network of technical libraries of the USSR was partially reconstructed, to the extent that the structure of control of the national economy was changed, economic administrative districts being enlarged and in some branches of industry state committees being created. By 1963, ninety central scientific and technical libraries of the Council of National Economy and eight public scientific and technical libraries of the Committee of the Council of Ministers of the Union Republics were functioning in 105 economic districts. In October 1964, their number was reduced to forty seven (in accordance with the number of enlarged economic districts). The majority of them were based on the central scientific and technical libraries of each Regional Economic Council, located in the towns and centres of the enlarged economic districts. Geographic branches arose on the basis of other central scientific and technical libraries of the Regional Councils, and functioned in the major industrial centres.

Some of the libraries serving branches of industry, including former branches of the state public scientific and technical library of the USSR, were transferred to the authority of the Central Institute of Information. The methodological functions were mainly entrusted to the central scientific and technical libraries of the Regional Economic Councils which encouraged the beginnings of systematic guidance in local inquiries and the use of new methods of working. The network of technical libraries in the administrative economic districts grew and developed. Advances were achieved with the cooperation and coordination in the activities of libraries of different systems and departments located in the area of a single economic district and the promotion of industrial, technical and economic literature was improved. However the technical libraries of various branches of industry, and similarly of the undertakings which they served, proved to be subordinate to the various Regional Economic Councils and therefore were unable to develop internal connections between themselves. The central scientific and technical libraries of the Regional Economic Councils, guiding all libraries irrespective of the branch to which they belonged, were unable to provide an equal service to all the libraries. The specific character of the library and bibliographic service offered by differing branches of industry was not always taken into account, and as a result the level of work in the libraries of various branches of industry differed.

The reorganisation of the control of industry on the branch principle, in accordance with the resolution of the September (1965) plenary meeting of the Central Committee of the Communist Party, entailed corresponding reorganisation of the network of technical libraries and began a new period in their development. The branch principle gave renewed life to the industrial library and bibliographic services. At present the basic links in the network of technical libraries are provided by the libraries of industrial undertakings which compose sixty seven percent of the total number of technical libraries (13·2 thousand with a book stock of 111 million printed items).

The organisational character of the libraries of industrial undertakings clearly show the specific attributes of Soviet technical libraries. Their essence is found in the principle that the library of an undertaking is connected with the production side and is a subdivision of the undertaking, where it functions and serves a relatively stable collective body in specific industrial conditions with literature and informational materials. This enables it to give on the one hand maximum operational help to the undertaking in fulfilment of its planned tasks and in the introduction of new techniques and advanced technology, and on the other to spread the influence of the library to the whole industrial collective and to each member of it.

In the program of the Communist Party, it is stated that technical progress considerably increases the demand for culture in industry and for special and general training of all workers.[13] The technical libraries of the country strive to encourage all engineers and other technical workers to read the specialist literature, and great advances have already been made in this direction. Thus, for example, in a Circassian factory for refrigerating equipment (Northern Caucasus) and in a Barnaul factory for mechanical presses (Altai territory), all the workers became readers in the works libraries. During the period of the all-Union inspection of technical libraries, carried out in honour of the fiftieth Anniversary of Soviet rule, planned efforts to increase the numbers of readers met with considerable success.

The specific character of the technical libraries in business undertakings determined their nature and form and their methods of work with readers. The basic problem was to enable the experience culled from the literature to be utilised by specific users. Great attention was paid to categories of readers such as innovators and inventors, members of the brigade of communist workers, front rank people in industry and young workers. In the resolution of the Central Committee of the Communist Party ' On the state of library affairs in the country and measures for improving them ' (1959), the necessity for the more active promotion of new techniques and the latest technology was indicated. Technical libraries began to allow readers opportunities for direct acquaintance with the literature and for independent choice of books. Among the more modern methods applied to work with readers are seminars for engineering and technical workers to examine new literature, the creation of review groups and information points, the compilation of bibliographic lists on current subjects for industry, and the promotion of library and bibliographical knowledge.

The system of open access by readers to book stocks, the organisation of branches, mobile and reference libraries in departments and industrial divisions, widened both the possibilities of demonstration and choice of the literature. Readers' problems are now satisfied to a much greater degree and the book stocks are used more extensively. Moreover it must especially be emphasised that a modern technical library is not limited to showing which publications are available. It informs readers of the value of each book and, by means of promoting the literature, participates in the introduction of new techniques and advanced technology into industry. It is noteworthy that in many undertakings the economic benefit obtained by calculating the introduction of innovations, drawn from technical literature, is estimated at many thousands of roubles. This is clear evidence of the fact that in the information system technical libraries occupy an important place. To cite only two examples: as a result of an investigation of technical literature and information material in the technical library, the collective body of the Gorlov engineering works of S M Kirov in 1965 introduced fifty recommendations, the economic effect of which amounted to 63,837 roubles. The library of the Grozny machine repair factory gave valuable help to its industry in 1965, the economic effect of which totalled 150,000 roubles.

A significant place in the network of technical libraries is occupied by the central scientific and technical library and its branches. These were established to cooperate with socialist industry, and were formulated as integral links in the national economy. Of thirty seven Union and Union republic industrial ministries at the present time, twenty six have central scientific and technical libraries covering branches of industry to which, together with library and bibliographic service, organisational and methodological guidance to all libraries of the corresponding branch of industry is entrusted. In order to widen their sphere of activity and to reach into every technical library, the central scientific and technical library branches organise reference or main libraries in the provinces based on the better libraries of industrial undertakings or geographic central scientific and technical libraries and their branches.

The major geographic central scientific and technical libraries and the libraries of republic importance normally enter into the library network of the country. They are in a way bases for several branches of industry in the service of books and bibliography to zones (regions, territories and republics), as well as being for the coordination of the work of libraries in different branches of industry and of different departments with technical literature. They are also methodological centres for the technical libraries of all systems and departments of a given territory. In the Russian Federation, the central scientific and technical libraries of the former Soviets of National Economy began to play the role of territorial central scientific and technical libraries. Up to the reorganisation they were subordinate to the Central Bureaux of Technical Information of the Regional Economic Council, and later were transferred to the State Committee of the Soviet Ministers of the USSR for Science and Technology. In Kazakhstan and the Baltic and Transcaucasian Republics, scientific and technical libraries and the libraries of the abolished Regional Economic Councils were transferred to the management of the State Planning Commissions, and the central scientific and technical libraries of the former Regional Economic Councils here became branches of the territorial scientific and technical libraries or reference libraries of branch ministries in the republics. By such an organisation, unified methodological guidance is achieved, the established ties are preserved and branch and territorial principles are combined in the best way.

The leading library, serving many branches of industry and the methodological centre for all the technical libraries of the country, is the State Public Scientific and Technical Library of the USSR. Eight years after its establishment, it became the centre of bibliographic work with literature on technical science and industrial production, and became a specialised scientific research institution in the field of library science and bibliography. The State Public Scientific and Technical Library of the USSR coordinates the working methods of the network of technical libraries and libraries of other systems.

The All-Union Patent Technical Library (created in 1924) and the Central Polytechnical Library play a fundamental part among technical libraries serving Soviet science and industry.[14] To the former was entrusted the task of collecting and handling the state patent stock of the USSR. The library served as a base for the examination of the latest achievements in technical concepts. Together with this, it is the methodological centre for problems of library work of all kinds with patent literature. In the stocks of the Central Polytechnical Library, functioning as a component of the all-Union society for science, pre-revolutionary Russian and Soviet technical literature, in the natural sciences and the history of technology, popular scientific books and also stocks of special forms of technical literature are more fully represented than in other libraries. The basic task of the Central Polytechnical Library is the promotion of scientific, technical and natural sciences among wide sections of the population.

Libraries of scientific research institutes, design offices and planning organisations, technical libraries of the Academies of Sciences of the USSR, Academies of Science of the Union Republics, branch academies, higher and intermediate special educational institutions, carry out a considerable amount of work.

The nature and forms of the work in technical libraries are subordinate to state problems, which determine the different stages of technical and economic development of the socialist industry of the country. In the new five-year plan, the technical libraries are commissioned to ensure operative library and bibliographic service to scientific staffs, to give the maximum help to the collections of business concerns and organisations in the most rapid technical re-equipping of the whole national economy.

The Twenty Third Congress of the Communist Party, in its resolution, emphasised that the construction of the material and technical foundation of communism depends to a large extent on a well placed, structural and reliable system of information ensuring exhaustive data ' on the results of scientific investigation being carried out in the country and abroad, also on the achievements of new methods of production and on patentable and innovational propositions '.[15] These Party instructions are embodied in the resolution of the Council of Ministers ' On the state system of scientific and technical information ', where the means for fundamental improvement are defined in the current five-year plan for scientific and technical information. Predominant attention is paid to the further development of a system of scientific and technical information in branches of industry as the basis of a state system, the coordination of the activities of all-Union information organisations of a branch or a variety of branches of industry and also of scientific and universal (state) libraries. The resolution requires the achievement of conformity in the combined work of technical libraries and information organisations, the elimination of duplication and the creation of a reference and information service based on common reference and information stocks. The measures outlined for increasing the effectiveness of scientific and technical information are directly concerned with technical libraries and demand improvement of all their activities in the interests of further modernisation of industry and the development of the national economy of our country. The instructions concerning the organisation of an interdepartmental commission attached to the State Committee for Science and Technology of Ministers on the coordination of the activities of special scientific and technical libraries have extremely important significance for the most active use of all means and methods of information. The necessity for technical libraries to establish maximum conformity between themselves and with libraries of other systems, departments and information organisations very strongly encourages accelerated and wholesale transfer of technical libraries to operation on the principle of a unified system of library and bibliographic service, based on the combination of specialisation and wide cooperation.[17] At present, a unified system of library and bibliographic service is considered not only from the

64

geographic library aspect, as up to now, but also from the branch aspect, which makes it possible to unify the technical libraries at all levels of all branches of industrial production on a nationwide scale, and the conformity in the work of libraries of different branches of industry on a republic, territorial, industrial district or town scale.

In the implementation of a unified library and bibliographic service to workers in industry, unified plans drawn up within the limits of the branch central scientific and technical libraries, and within the boundaries of a definite territory by the central scientific and technical libraries, the central libraries of technical information of the economic districts, and the district scientific libraries of the State Planning Commissions of the Union republics are of assistance. The draft plans of the leading libraries, heading the branch groups of libraries within economic districts (republics) form the basis of the unified plans. The branch central scientific and technical libraries determine the major direction of library and bibliographic service to the branch as a whole. The plans of the leading libraries of different branches of industry within one economic district make it possible, with the territorial central scientific and technical libraries and the central libraries for technical information in the economic districts, to accomplish inter-branch coordination and cooperation in the activities of libraries of various branches of industry in the given territorial sub-division.

Coordination and cooperation, both in the inner network and in the inter-network scale, provide unified methodological guidance to all the technical libraries of the country. It is necessary to develop a general direction for the activity of technical libraries, to secure their close ties with libraries of other systems and departments having collections of technical literature. This is only possible by the establishment of a system of methodological guidance to technical libraries so that each link will gradually carry on the most important principles among libraries of its network, and when the direction and methods of work of every structural subdivision of the system and the sphere of contact of different library centres are clearly defined.

The system of institutions for methodological guidance to technical libraries through the principle of branch control of the national economy may be represented in the following way: the State Scientific and Technical Library of the USSR—central scientific and technical libraries of one branch of industry or of many branches—head libraries, guiding the branch groups of libraries in various economic districts. Such a construction permits the creation of a harmonious system of interconnected methodological centres and efficiently fulfils the task of giving direct help to any library.

The implementation of a unified system of library and bibliographic service to industry—one of the main directions in the solution of the national problem of a unified system of library and bibliographic service to the whole population of the country—must not be merely local. In the introduction of the new system, the implementation of the following measures will be helped everywhere by: a) the rational distribution of libraries (and in the first place, of technical libraries) in the territories of the USSR, the securing of technical libraries for each branch of industry, the creation of libraries in all industrial undertakings with more than 1,000 workers, the introduction of mobile and reference stocks for industrial undertakings with a smaller number and without further prospects of growth; b) the examination of the reader complement and clear differentiation of reader categories among libraries participating in a unified system and information organisations; c) the creation, with the help of research and general libraries and information organisations, of unified organisational and methodological documentation, which defines the place of every type of technical library and serves as a basis for the introduction of a unified system on a national scale, the reviewing of the methods of a number of processes, and the development of suggestions for new theoretical methods in connection with problems which arise; d) the development of resources and the raising of the general level of work of each individual technical library.

Thus the path taken by technical libraries during fifty years of Soviet rule conclusively indicates that technical libraries provide one of the most important library networks of our country, structurally and functionally designed. They have many millions of books at their disposal together with large numbers of readers, qualified library staff and rich experience of specialised forms and methods of work.

The network of Soviet technical libraries embraces the library service at all levels in the direction of industry in all its branches. At every stage of the technical and economic development of the country, new forms and methods of work with technical literature appeared and new types of libraries arose. Library service to Soviet industry is accomplished in different ways in response to the character and range of the activities served and by means of the creation of differently formed types of technical libraries.

Currently there is a unified system of library and bibliographic service to workers in industry which encourages the reading of professional literature. This is introduced both territorially and also on the branch principle. The introduction of a unified system must be considered as a double sided process: on one hand, it considerably assists in raising the level of work in every individual technical library, and on the other hand it serves as a pledge of successful library service to industry as a whole.

LITERATURE REFERENCES AND NOTES

1 All-Union library census, 1 October, 1934, pages 156-307. TIM, 1936.

2 For more details *see*: S M Kulikov (The demand for books on applied science) *Byulleteni obshchestva elektrotekhnikov,* 1913, *85,* pages 378-381; *86,* pages 393-397.

3 (Protocol of the meeting of the Soviet Society on 4 September 1913) *Byulleteni obshchestva elektrotekhnikov,* 1913, *96,* page 540.

4 D Bedsole: A library survey of 117 corporations. *Special libraries* (NY) 1963, *54* (10), pages 615-622.

5 E Winter: Special libraries and technical information. East and West. *Special libraries* (NY), 1962, *53* (4), pages 194-198.

6 The following papers are devoted to the development of the network of technical libraries: F I Karatygin: *Tipy i set tekhnicheskikh bibliotek* (Types and network of technical libraries) Dissertation defended in Moscow, State Library Institute, 1948; M M Vinokur, and others: (Technical libraries as an assistance in the service to industry and transport) in *Bibliotechnoe delo v SSSR. Sbornik statei* (Library affairs in the USSR. Collected papers), pages

141-179. Moscow, 1957; E N Morozova: (The creation of a unified network of scientific and technical libraries), *Sovetskaya bibliografiya*, 1962, *52*, pages 81-83.

7 For more details *see*: L A Shlossberg: *Ocherk istorii GNB* (Outline of the history of the State Scientific Library), Moscow, Arkhiv GNB, 1930; F I Karatygin: *Istoriya Gosudarstvennoi nauchnoi biblioteki* (History of the State Scientific Library), Moscow, Arkhiv GNB, 1947.

8 (Collected documents on Party and Soviet publications) *Pravda*, pages 414-415, Moscow, 1954.

9 *Pervoe soveshchanie bibliotek tyazheloi promyshlennosti. Rezolyutsii i postanovleniya* (The first conference of libraries of heavy industries. Resolutions and decisions), pages 6-10. Moscow, 1933; *Materialy soveshchaniya opornykh otraslevykh bibliotek tyazheloi promyshlennosti* (The conference of reference libraries in branches of the heavy industries) 26-31 January 1929. Moscow, State Scientific Library, 1930.

10 R P Kharitonov: (Libraries of the State Scientific and Technical Committees and Regional Economic Councils for the assistance of industry) *Biblioteki SSSR Opyt raboty*, 1960, *13*, pages 75-91.

11 *Sbornik rukovodyashchikh materialov po bibliotechnoi rabote* (Collection of informative material on library work), pages 17-20. Moscow, 1963.

12 A V Kremenetskaya: *Gosudarstvennaya publichnaya nauchno-tekhnicheskaya biblioteka SSSR* (The State Public Scientific and Technical Library of the USSR) 1959-1963. Moscow, 1965.

13 (Program of the Communist Party of the Soviet Union) *Pravda*, page 67. Moscow, 1961.

14 The stocks of the library of the Polytechnical Museum (created in 1872) and of the library of the Society of students of natural science, anthropology and ethnography (created in 1864) formed the basis of this library.

15 *Materialy XXIII's ezda KPSS* (Matters of the Twenty-Third Congress of the Communist Party of the Soviet Union), page 127. Moscow, Polizdat, 1966.

16 *Sobranie postanovlenii pravitel'stva SSSR* (Collection of the resolutions of the Government of the USSR), page 220. Moscow, 1966, (25).

17 For details *see*: B N Bachaldin (A unified system of library and bibliographic service to industry—a wide road) *Biblioteki SSSR. Opyt raboty*, 1964, *27*, pages 19-31; O S Chubar'yan: (On the problem of a unified system of library and bibliographic service to industry) *Tekhnicheskie biblioteki SSSR*, 1963 (5) pages 3-7.

V THE LIBRARY NETWORK OF THE ACADEMY OF SCIENCES OF THE USSR

by B N BACHALDIN

THE NEW ASPECT OF THE LIBRARY

Half a century has passed since Lenin, examining the unique collection of books and manuscripts in the Library of the Academy of Sciences, said ' What enormous riches and how necessary all this is!'.[1] These words of Lenin started the program of library development and determined the new attitude of the Academy of Sciences to the organisation of library work after the October Revolution.

It is widely known that the roots of the library network of the Academy of Sciences date from the beginning of the eighteenth century. But the Great October Revolution formed the boundary between the past and the present and radically changed the whole outlook of the Academy library. To understand the essence of these changes, it would be helpful to recall the position of the libraries in the Academy of Sciences in 1917.

The libraries were independent, had been developed irregularly, and were totally uncoordinated, being under the influence of the narrowly specialised interest of one or two scholars and leading scientific institutions.

The selective character of the Academy libraries was most consistently manifest in their day to day work, directed mainly to satisfying the inquiries of only a narrow circle of academic readers. The stocks of the libraries were little used, although some of them possessed valuable collections, having been formed with the direct participation of great scholars who influenced the choice of literature, and who endowed considerable sums for acquisitions and bequeathed personal collections. Thus the stocks of scientific literature should be regarded as a most important part of the heritage received by the Academy of Sciences after the victory of the Great October Socialist Revolution.[2]

The modern Academy library is an integral part of the state library system for scientific and technical information and fulfils a responsible and varied role. In every possible way it assists the communist structure in our country in the development of science

70

and culture and with the education of scientific staff. The library successfully operates as the scientific and technical information bureau of the Academy of Sciences and carries out considerable work in the distribution and promotion of scientific knowledge to the mass of the population.

The Soviet Academy library is closely connected with service to scientific research institutions. By being aware of the range of inquiries in its own institute, research station, museum or observatory and their current and long-term plans, each library at the same time is a part of the library system of the Academy and is therefore always in touch with the basic problems of science. Through mutual use of the collections and of the reference, bibliographic and information tools, the Academy libraries managed to organise a deep and varied service to readers, and to become an integral unit of the scientific institutions.

After 1917 the Academy of Sciences, as a higher scientific organisation, began to actively help in the socialistic reconstruction of the country.

The process of research is very complex. Books play an essential role in creative scientific work, experiments and discoveries, the world's scientific literature becoming wider and richer year by year. Only libraries are capable of providing all the necessary material for study. This was always understood in the Academy of Sciences but it was only during the years of Soviet rule that the real prerequisites were created for the gradual and enormous development of the whole network of libraries (planned financing, replenishment of stocks of foreign literature, major bibliographic works, etc).

The progress of the modern Academy library was irregular, since the development of the Academy of Sciences itself was not easy. Its fine pre-revolution establishments, sometimes very weakly linked to the vital interests of the people, were changed into institutes with new tasks and potentialities and with a considerable number of scientific co-workers. In spite of the difficulties the government formed eight new institutes (for example, institutes dealing with physico-chemical analysis, platinum, physiology and soil science), from 1917 to 1927, and the number of workers increased from 220 to 1,500.[3]

It is natural that the ever increasing importance of science, brought about by the revolution, also found its reflection in library affairs, for it brought library work into a new prominence and put forward new aims and tasks for its development.

THE FORMATION OF THE LIBRARY SYSTEM OF THE ACADEMY OF SCIENCES OF THE USSR

The library network of the Academy of Sciences, which began to be formed long before 1917, was faced for the first time during Soviet rule with the following fundamental problems: how to use the book resources inherited from the past to the best advantage, by which paths and on which principles and organisational bases to develop library and bibliographical service to Soviet science and in particular to scientific groups of Academy institutions. To put the problem in perspective it must be remembered that in 1917 the Academy contained no more than fifteen departmental* libraries. However the major Academy library (founded in 1714) which always preserved the role of the central library, and which worked unco-ordinated with other libraries, was faced with the problem of establishing a planned, organised and unified network of libraries and the provision of a service to science through the stocks contained within them.

We must remember those librarians and directors of the Academy who, during the first years of Soviet rule, determined the correct course of development for science libraries, based on a combination of centralisation and decentralisation and ensuring the most rational and economically suitable organisation of library service. At the same time as modernising the service to readers in the Academy's institutions, the objective was to unite the separate Academy libraries organisationally, to centralise the separate forms of library work and to enable stocks held in separate libraries to be easily retrievable. Such a decision was dictated since separately the individual libraries were already unable to satisfy the continuously growing demands of readers for scientific literature. The position of the newly created scientific institutions in the Academy, opening libraries in new areas, was especially difficult.

*(Here and throughout this chapter the term 'departmental' has been substi-tuted for 'special' in this context as being more indicative of the organisa-tional relationships—*editor*).

It is understandable that the aim of developing departmental libraries and the creation of a unified and planned library organisation within the limits of the system of institutes could not be realised immediately. It was necessary not only to solve the organisational problems but also to overcome the psychological barriers raised by the separatist frame of mind found in the staff of some departmental libraries, frequently encouraged by scientific co-workers.

In 1925, the Library of the Academy of Sciences made a proposal for the unification of methods of cataloguing in the Academy libraries network and compiled a union catalogue of all its own book stocks. This was the simplest form of cooperation, not affecting the rights of the separate libraries. The creation of the library network was rightly connected with the establishment of a stocktaking procedure of library resources. The idea of a union catalogue, covering the whole stock, received approval in the Academy libraries.[4] The problem of the planned acquisition of foreign publications and their distribution between the central and departmental libraries in the separate institutions was solved.

In accordance with the instruction of the Academy of Sciences the central library of the Academy examined, in 1926, twenty four Leningrad departmental libraries.[5] It became clear how different the libraries were in size (from a few hundred to tens of thousands of volumes) and how they differed in the organisation of their work. In the libraries of the Botanical Museum (20 thousand volumes), of the Zoological Museum (50 thousand volumes), of the Pushkin Museum (120 thousand volumes) there were qualified library workers, but in small libraries the scientific workers carried out library duties at the same time as their scientific work. These and other libraries needed methodological guidance and help from the specialists of a central library. That is why in considering the results of the inspection, representatives of the Library of the Academy of Sciences and co-workers in departmental libraries supported the establishment of firm and efficient ties between the departmental libraries and the central library and amongst themselves without sacrificing administrative autonomy.[6] The idea of centralisation found reflection in the temporary rules of the Libraries of the Academy of Sciences, developed in 1926. In them, departmental libraries were considered essentially as branches of the central library.

73

The basis of the plan for the organisation of library affairs in the Academy of Sciences (1928) was primarily the idea of a common library stock for the Academy of Sciences, distributed in accordance with the scientific research work between the central and departmental libraries.[7] However there was no success in the achievement of a system of affiliation for the departmental libraries in the Academy of Sciences in the twenties. The temporary rules and the basic propositions remained to all intents and purposes merely declarations since they were not developed by organisational measures.

Drastic changes were made in 1931 when twelve departmental libraries were transferred to the category of branches. The central library began to acquire stocks for them and to catalogue their current holdings, as well as enrolling the co-workers of these libraries onto its staff.[8] In fact then eight further libraries began to work as branches and subsequently this process continued. In the thirties, the Library of the Academy of Sciences began to give regular organisational and methodologic help to the departmental libraries (planning and accounts, control and consultation).

CHANGES IN THE GEOGRAPHY OF THE LIBRARY NETWORK

The industrialisation of the country and collectivisation of farming caused further developments in scientific research and a widening of the network of scientific institutions, especially after 1934 when, in accordance with a Government decision, the Academy of Sciences of the USSR was transferred to Moscow. In order to ensure close connection between science and the practice of socialist development, a division for technology was created in the structure of the Academy in 1935. The thirties were remarkable for intensive growth in the network and the reorganisation of a number of scientific institutions devoted to the humanities. To concentrate scientific effort in a common centre and increase the level of research work in the social sciences, all the institutes of the Communist Academy, founded in 1918 on Lenin's instructions, were transferred in 1936 to the Academy of Sciences of the USSR.

The discovery of the natural resources of the Far East, Siberia, the Far North, Kazakhstan, the creation of industry, and the development of agriculture demanded broad participation by science in the evaluation of these resources and in the development of plans for their use in the national economy. These tasks were accomplished by the complex of scientific institutions of the Academy of Sciences of the USSR, which formed bases and branches in 1932-1934 in the Kola peninsula, in the Far East, the Urals, in Kazakhstan, Tajikistan and Transcaucasia.

In the thirties, working contacts between the institutions of the Academy of Sciences and the departmental libraries were even more strongly developed. The principles of centralisation, developed in the twenties and evaluated at the beginning of the thirties in the experience of a small number of Leningrad Academy libraries, could now be applied to the whole system of Academy libraries, geographically separated and deeply differentiated in subject. (It was necessary to take strong measures for this if only partially to surmount the difficulties arising from the move of the Academy of Sciences to Moscow, which affected library service to the scientific institutions of the metropolis because the books were mainly housed in Leningrad.) Eleven special libraries concerned with physical and natural sciences, mathematics and technology were transferred to Moscow and formed the Moscow library network of the Academy of Sciences.[9] Their total stock originally amounted to only 180 thousand volumes (now about 12 million).

The direction of the Moscow network was entrusted to a specially created temporary library station.[10] It was conceived as an intermediary between the Library of the Academy of Sciences and the Moscow departmental libraries for natural sciences and technology until such time as all the institutions of the Academy of Sciences would move into the capital. However its function gradually changed since the Library of the Academy was not transferred to Moscow. Operative leadership of the Moscow departmental libraries from Leningrad was not possible and the station was changed from a temporary organ to an independent centre of the Academy, a part of the network, not having its own book stocks, not serving readers directly and formally subordinate to the Library of the Academy of Sciences in Leningrad.

During the first period of activity of the Moscow libraries (1934-1936), their removal from the Leningrad collections of the Academy of Sciences was very deeply felt, especially in the field of biological sciences since the greatest collection of biological literature was concentrated in Leningrad. Moreover it was necessary to satisfy the demand of the new scientific research institutes of the Academy of Sciences, which were created in 1934-1936 and did not have book collections at their disposal. These circumstances induced the Library of the Academy of Sciences and the temporary library station to strengthen the stocks of the Moscow network: the Library of the Academy of Sciences transferred part of its stock to Moscow and the temporary library station acquired some valuable private book collections. In parallel with this the work of interlibrary loans was expanded and stimulated. The measures taken gave positive results: the role of the Moscow network of departmental libraries increased, and in 1935 their book loans were greater than the total issues in the Leningrad departmental libraries.

Beginning in 1932, one of the primary tasks of the central library became the organisation of the libraries in the branches of the Academy of Sciences of the USSR. The duplicated and unused stocks of the Library of the Academy of Sciences were urgently reviewed and a considerable part was distributed between the libraries of the branches. The central library set about systematic acquisitions and organisation and methodological assistance to these libraries. In 1931-34 the Library of the Academy of Sciences, and later also the temporary library station, gradually transferred the whole network of libraries to centralised acquisitions, both of Soviet and of foreign literature and to the initial processing of publications for all the departmental libraries (except the libraries in the branches), releasing them from laborious technical processes and allowing them to concentrate their energy on service to readers.

AMALGAMATION OF THE LIBRARIES OF THE TWO ACADEMIES

A decisive moment in the history of library development in the Academy of Sciences of the USSR was the amalgamation of its libraries with the libraries of the Communist Academy which had not only great organisational importance but also political importance.

The library system of the Communist Academy was set up with unprecedented speed and did not expend energy in overcoming and solving library problems (although a poorly established structural organisation was permitted). For example, up to 1928 the value of departmental libraries was underestimated, and an attempt to satisfy the inquiries of all the research institutions of the Communist Academy through the main library predominated. The supporters of such a concentrated service saw departmental libraries at most as ' improvised libraries with a minimal quantity of books of purely reference value '.[11]

At the same time, the rapid change in the position of the Communist Academy institutions gave impetus to the development of separatist tendencies, especially in libraries which operated independently and joined the network later. They objected to the guidance from the centre and considered complete autonomy the main prerequisite for the organisation of service to scientific co-workers in their institute. The central library of the Communist Academy was obliged to defend patiently and insistently the principle of the unity of the network and to continue the struggle against separatist policies. Setting itself the task of aiding the research work of all the institutes in the Communist Academy, the central library justified the necessity for active and unified guidance to all the library units in the Academy, and considered that only by such means was it possible to avoid duplication in work, the dissipation of resources, the coordination of the interests of the separate institutes and the establishment of efficient mutual relations between the library and the institute.

At the end of the twenties the central library of the Communist Academy succeeded in developing a network of departmental libraries. It transferred the literature in its stocks to the departmental libraries according to their interests and organised centralised acquisition of current publications. Thus, the stocks of the libraries of the following institutes were replenished through the direct participation of the central library; the Institute of Philosophy (1932), the Institute of Economics (1930) and the Institute of Soviet Construction (1925) and a number of other institutions. In order for the stocks to be used even more fully and effectively, the Central Library of the Communist Academy, in the thirties, frequently made temporary transfers of individual titles and whole series to the research institutions. In this way, the growth of two forms of service in the V P Volgin Fundamental Library of Social Science of the Academy of Sciences of the USSR was encouraged: the display

77

of current material and the transfer to departmental libraries for protracted use of valuable (predominantly foreign) literature, selected by the central library in accordance with the subject interests of the corresponding research institution.

Reconstruction of the central library with branches in the first half of the thirties (previously a subject structure had existed) greatly helped all forms of inter-library cooperation in the Communist Academy. For example, with the creation of branch bibliographic sections (history, economics, etc) very favourable conditions were established for a joint (central and departmental) bibliographic service to research institutions. In previous years the central library of the Communist Academy carried out reference and bibliographic work solely for inquiries from the separate institutions. After 1934 it reconstructed the work, anticipating demand and gradually transferring to the compilation of informational and retrospective lists to the research plans of the institutes.

Therefore at the time of amalgamation with the library system of the Academy of Sciences of the USSR, the relationships between the libraries of the Communist Academy were fixed and the functions of service to research institutions were distributed amongst them.

With the inclusion of the library network of the Communist Academy in the unified library system, the forms and problems of library work, the type of stock acquisition and the subjects of book exhibitions were changed fundamentally. The Academy of Sciences also contained libraries previously connected with the humanities, but the classical sciences (ancient history, archaeology and philology) were their predominant interest. The institutes of the Communist Academy were concerned with the study of theoretical problems of Marxism, the most urgent problems of politics, political economy, the development of a working international communist movement, world economy and the internal politics of the USSR and foreign countries.

The combination of the library networks also promoted a considerable broadening of the readership, including co-workers of institutions outside the Academy. Bibliographic information began to be guided not only by the inquiries of Academy institutes but also by many branches of science as a whole.

The combination of the two great systems of research libraries entailed certain difficulties. The diversified and manifold scientific research institutions of the Academy of Sciences, their geographical ramifications, the extensiveness of their book resources (about 10 million volumes) and the importance of the task of service to the greatest scientific institution of the country made it necessary to solve complex organisational problems. No academy or university in the world had such a vast network of institutes or possessed so great a stock. A rapid effort was made to draw up regulations for the coordination of activities of the Academy libraries, for defining the interrelationships between the Moscow and Leningrad libraries of the network, assigning to them duties concerning service to the research activities of the Academy of Sciences and for organising guidance to the whole library network.

The library of the Communist Academy changed its name in 1936 to the Fundamental Library of the Division of Social Science of the Academy of Sciences of the USSR, but found itself in a very difficult position after amalgamation. Some of the institutes, which it had earlier served, widened the range of their activities and became part of the Academy of Sciences (for example, the Institute of History). The Fundamental Library together with the departmental libraries under its jurisdiction had to serve those branches of the Social Sciences which had had a secondary significance for the library of the Communist Academy (archaeology, ethnography, literary science, oriental studies). Similar widening of activities did not take place in the Leningrad network of Academy libraries, although the reform of 1936 also posed important organisational and technical problems (in particular guidance to the section's network in Moscow).

After the transfer of a number of the Academy institutes to Moscow and the creation of a network of departmental libraries there, an attempt was made to examine in theory the network and to find the most rational solution to the organisational problems of the library system of the Academy of Sciences. In a resolution on 5 December 1936, the Praesidium of the Academy of Sciences set up a special commission under the chairmanship of Academician I V Grebenshchikov consisting of scholars (mainly from the academies) and representatives of both central libraries.[12]

The special feature and at the same time the weakness of the plan for the organisation of library affairs in the Academy consisted of its future orientation as a united Moscow based system of libraries. But even from the beginning doubt was generated among the members of the commission on the advisability of the transfer of the Library of the Academy of Sciences to Moscow. As time showed these doubts were justified. The necessity existed for the organisation of a library service to the scientific institutes in Moscow and in Leningrad. Neither the Academy of Sciences nor its book stock was transferred completely to Moscow. The conclusions of the commission are therefore interesting in theory but virtually without any practical applications. As before, there were two library centres, each acting on its own. The direction became much more complicated with the growing network in Moscow of departmental libraries in natural sciences and technology. An organisation of management control of the libraries in Moscow became necessary.

The Praesidium of the Academy of Sciences made some attempt in 1938-1940 to find a more successful organisational form of interrelationship between the integral parts of the library system. But not one of the ideas stood up to practical use. Meanwhile the network of Moscow departmental libraries in natural sciences and technology became virtually an independent unit with merely formal submission to Leningrad. It must be mentioned that the centre of aid to the Academy libraries in the other city nevertheless moved from Leningrad to Moscow. This was very important because the conditions for closer ties between the Leningrad libraries and the centre were established mainly for more effective and satisfactory centralised supply of library literature. In February 1940, in Moscow, a group of co-workers was specially selected for work with the branch libraries which at first was only concerned with the current acquisitions for eight of the more remote libraries. Subsequently help to libraries of the other city was considerably expanded.

During the five years (1936-1941) preceding the war further development of the library network of the Academy of Sciences took place and the idea of centralisation received final acknowledgement, and the organisational and guiding role of both library centres (Moscow and Leningrad) was strengthened. It is true that there was no clear and precise plan for the organisation of the library network in the Academy of Sciences at that time, just as there was also no systematic control beyond implementation of the resolutions taken.

THE LIBRARY NETWORK OF THE ACADEMY OF SCIENCES IN 1941-1955
The war with fascist Germany upset the normal development of many libraries of the Academy and slowed the organisation of the network and the coordination of work in all its sections. But these processes did not completely cease however, and under the influence of the war, they rapidly changed their character and extent. During those difficult years the most valuable stocks of the Academy libraries were evacuated to the interior of the country, their replenishment with current home and foreign publications was adjusted and coordinated, international book exchange was maintained and any serious problems in the stocks of the scientific literature were avoided. The majority of the libraries of the Academy carried on the service to readers.[13]

Overcoming many difficulties in the war period, the Academy of Sciences of the USSR created, in 1943-1944, seven new departmental libraries among which were those attached to the Scientific Research Base of the Academy in the Komi Autonomous Soviet Socialist Republic, the Marine Hydro-physical Institute and the Forestry Institute.

During the first post-war years efforts were directed first of all to the repair of library buildings which had suffered, to the replacement of stocks, to work on the book collections, which had been withdrawn from use during air raids and gunfire, to the restoration of former stocks, and to the establishment of new book exchange agreements with foreign scientific institutions. A considerable number of publications were selected from spare stocks in Academy libraries to restore damaged or destroyed libraries in territories occupied by fascist troops. Spare stocks were also widely used for setting up libraries in new scientific research institutes of the Academy of Sciences of the USSR, which arose in various towns.

The library network of the Academy of Sciences proceeded to grow unceasingly as one of the results of the progress of science. Already by the autumn of 1945, seven new departmental libraries were created, then six in 1946 and seven in 1947. According to incomplete data, from 1948-1955, about fifty departmental libraries were opened. The typical characteristics of the development of Soviet science in the fifties—development of complex problems in mathematics, mechanics, physics, chemistry, electronics, automation and atomic energy—were reflected in their work.

In the last twenty years, the main variety has become not a branch departmental library, but a library of 'problem' form serving institutions, concerned with work on currently pressing problems in modern science. Thus, for example, there are departmental libraries of the Institutes for the Chemistry of Silicates (1948), of Macro Molecular Compounds (1949), of Semiconductors (1952) and the Laboratory of Anisotropic Structures (1953). A 'problem' library is different in that it needs a more systematic specialised book stock, clear definition and a wealth of reference, bibliographic and information works for assistance with research problems.

Another characteristic in the development of the network of Academy libraries in the post-war period was the appearance of numerous libraries in various regions of the country.

The intensive growth of the library network demanded immediate solution to the organisational problems such as space, acquisition of stocks, staff and finance. Nevertheless, beginning as early as 1945, the central libraries prepared and carried out many important joint measures directed towards more active use of stocks, better production of information about literature, development of bibliographic work and inter-library exchanges. From the end of the forties, the guiding role of the central libraries of the Academy of Sciences was strengthened and their organisational and methodological work became especially diversified in nature and varied in form.

In 1945, the Central libraries organised two exhibitions, devoted to the printed scientific publications of the Academy of Sciences during the 220 years of its existence. One of the exhibitions was shown in the Fundamental Library of Social Sciences and the other in the Library of the Academy of Sciences in Leningrad. Both exhibitions, organised in the last year of the war, were serious political events and a persuasive demonstration of the triumph of socialist ideology and the colossal role of Soviet science in social progress. The exhibitions, as successful experiments in the combination of resources, were joint Academy measures achieved through the coordinating and organisational role of the central libraries and with the active participation of departmental libraries.

The consolidation of the efforts of the libraries of branches of the Academy was actively promoted by conferences of their chiefs convened from 1951 onwards,[15] and also conferences of the Moscow libraries of the system (1954-1959). The conferences encouraged better acquaintance with the state of the libraries and their requirements, in order that they may have prompt and precise methodological and organisational assistance. Thus, a stock check was carried out, arrangement was improved, records were put in order, library soviets were created, the bibliographical service was improved and further plans made.

Although bibliographic work was widely developed in the Academy library network after the war, it was not coordinated to the fullest extent and cases of unjustified duplication arose. Nevertheless from 1948 to 1955, certain improvements were contemplated, namely that central libraries should either prepare bibliographies together with the departmental libraries or coordinate this work. For example, three volumes of indexes on natural history were compiled and published by the Fundamental Library and the Institute of Natural History. The departmental libraries participated in the preparation of an information bulletin *Nauka i nauchno-issledovatel'skaya rabota za rubezhom* (Science and scientific research work from abroad), published by the Fundamental Library of Social Sciences. Coordinated by the central libraries, bibliographies on certain branches of knowledge and separate subjects were compiled solely by the departmental libraries. Bibliographies of this kind were compiled by the libraries of the Institute of Law and the Institute of World Literature. It is possible to name many major subject works by the departmental libraries—for example the bibliographies on dielectrics (published as a separate book in 1952), on meteorites (printed in the journal *Meteoritika* (Meteorites) volume *9*, 1951, and on Pushkin's works.

From the end of the forties the library system of the Academy of Sciences of the USSR paid greatly increased attention to the problems of coordination of their work with the work of the libraries of the

Academies of Sciences in the Union republics. This type of library, which was created as the result of continual implementation of Leninist national policies, ensured a golden age of culture and science for the whole population of the Soviet Union and in a short time became major information and cultural centres for research. In the Academies of Sciences of the Union republics, fourteen central, over 180 departmental and twenty five branch libraries are in operation. With more than 20 million volumes available in their stocks, these libraries annually serve about 85 thousand scientific workers (37 thousand workers in the academies) and issue to them over 5 million volumes and periodical articles.

During the years of Soviet rule the libraries of the Academies of Sciences of the Union republics increased the qualified national staff of librarians and bibliographers and produced a national bibliography.

The libraries of the Academies of Sciences of the Union republics were always closely connected with the libraries of the Academy of Sciences of the USSR, and were constantly guided by them. Many of them in fact took their origin from libraries of branches of the Academy of Sciences of the USSR.

The influence of the library system of the Academy of Sciences of the USSR on the development of the library system of the Academies of Sciences of the Union republics is felt in all aspects. In particular there is recognition of the idea of centralisation of acquisition and processing of literature and the coordination of service. However at present typical contacts are based on mutual resources, exchange of library experience, coordination of library work, exchange of publications, inter-library loans and joint consultations. For example, the Fundamental Library of Social Sciences coordinated the preparation of such fundamental bibliographic works as *Slavyanskoe yazykoznanie* (Slav linguistics) and *Obshchee yazykonznanie* (General philology).[15] In addition to the bibliographers of this library, bibliographers of the libraries of the Academy of Sciences of the Ukrainian SSR and of the Academy of Sciences of the Belorussian SSR compiled the first edition, and twelve academies (the libraries of the Academies of Sciences of the Georgian and Turkmen SSRs did not participate) helped with the second.

In 1949 the tradition of joint conferences of libraries of the

Academy of Sciences of the USSR and of the Academies of Sciences of the Union republics began. The importance of the nine conferences held up to the present consists of the coordination of work in libraries of the same type, the dissemination of the latest experience and the extension of the influence of the library system of the Academy of Sciences of the USSR on the library affairs in the Union republics.

From 1948 to 1962, the Library of the Academy of Sciences in Leningrad and the Fundamental Library of Social Sciences together issued a joint classified catalogue *Novaya inostrannaya kniga v bibliotekakh Akademii nauk SSSR* (New foreign books in the libraries of the Academy of Sciences of the USSR), which reflected the literature received in all libraries of the system of the Academy of Sciences, and from 1950 also reflected the books of the libraries of the republic academies. With the participation of the Moscow departmental libraries in natural sciences and technology a union catalogue was created in 1947-1948, listing the stocks of foreign literature, and in 1953 a union catalogue of the Soviet literature was begun.

The period 1948-1955 is notable for the considerably strengthened interest by the guiding agents of the Academy—the Praesidia and the library commissions—in the organisation of library affairs. Commissions were established, which examined the position in the Academy libraries. Many resolutions of the Praesidia led to improvements in the structure of the library network of the Academy, strengthening its guidance and increasing the effectiveness of the use of the accumulated book resources.[16] Resolutions were also taken concerning individual problems of library work.

Problems of an organisational and legal character were the objects of special attention by the Praesidium of the Academy of Sciences of the USSR and the Library Commission, but so long as the interlibrary relations of the Academy are spontaneous, being based on two opposite principles—centralisation and decentralisation—the production of standard documents is difficult. During the ten postwar years they did not consider further the numerous projects, regulations and suggestions relating to the activity of the library network as a whole and of its separate links (departmental and central libraries).

After the Twentieth Congress of the Communist Party the library network of the Academy of Sciences of the USSR entered into a new period of development and although still far from being typical, the signs are fully apparent, though some basic tendencies in the development of the USSR during 1956-1967 can be mentioned.

The course taken by the Party in coping with the effects of new sources of raw materials, fuel, electrical energy, especially in the eastern areas of the country and in the creation of powerful new industrial areas, demanded many kinds of scientific development. In complete conformity with scientific progress after 1956 and in connection with the formation of outlying centres of the Academy of Sciences of the USSR, the library network of the Academy entered into a new era of its development. Large new departmental libraries appeared at different ends of the country (in Adler, the Komsomol Kuibyshev district, Krasnoyarsk and Stavropol). The earlier existing Academy libraries are also being developed, first of all those of the branches. They are more intensively supplementing their stocks, perfecting catalogues and methods of library and bibliographic service to scientific institutes, very often starting fundamental bibliographic work organising mobile libraries and helping the libraries of affiliated institutes.

In 1957, in accordance with the resolution of the Soviet government, a powerful scientific centre began to be formed near Novosibirsk, namely the Novosibirsk Division of the Academy of Sciences of the USSR. It is composed of the scientific institutes of Western Siberia, Eastern Siberia, Yakutia and the Far Eastern branches of the Academy of Sciences of the USSR, and to it were subordinated the Sakhalin composite scientific research institute and other scientific institutions distributed in the immense territories from the Urals to the Pacific Ocean. Even now an investigation of the more than sixty scientific institutions, universities and botanical gardens is being carried out. The scientific staff of the Siberian branch represents a large and constantly growing army of scholars.

Up to 1957, the Academy institutions of Siberia maintained a total of nine libraries, with small stocks and publications. Even the composite libraries of the branches of the Academy had no more than 100-150 thousand volumes. The Siberian scholars were frequently forced to go to Moscow, in order to consult libraries. In creating the Siberian division, the Praesidium of the Academy of Sciences of the USSR provided a library and bibliographic base in the Siberian complex of scientific libraries.

At the beginning of 1957, the Eastern division of the Library of the Academy of Sciences of the USSR[17] was organised. At first its purpose was very limited, namely serving the branches of the Academy of Sciences in Siberia and the Far East. But in connection with the organisation, in July 1957, of the Siberian division of the Academy this new library was forced to take upon itself service to all the scientific institutes of the Siberian division and also to the scientific institutions of other departments. Such a tremendous scale of work demanded comprehensive development of the Eastern division. In September 1957 the library of the Western Siberian branch of the Academy was attached to it and the library of the Academy of Sciences and its system extensively supplied it with literature. It is characteristic that a stock of 149 thousand volumes was accumulated in thirteen years in the library of the Western Siberian branch. This stock was doubled in two years when it was transformed into the Eastern division of the Leningrad Library of the Academy of Sciences.

In the large towns of Siberia, especially in Novosibirsk, from 1957 (as formerly in Leningrad and Moscow) the library and bibliographic service to the system of scientific institutions of the Siberian division was differentiated, and complexes of departmental libraries were formed. At present departmental libraries of eighteen institutes are functioning in Novosibirsk alone, and the total in the Siberian division of the Academy of Sciences of the USSR amounts to over sixty. The need for a Novosibirsk provincial guidance centre becomes very much more obvious since the guidance is from Leningrad or Moscow.

The Eastern division of the Library of the Academy of Sciences fulfilled some functions of a central library in Novosibirsk.[18] However another library (the State Scientific Library of the Ministry of Higher Education of the USSR) was predestined to become the present centre, possessing almost four million specialised items of Soviet and foreign literature on technology and natural sciences. The prospect of obtaining a valuable stock so closely related to the needs of the Siberian division caused the leaders of the Academy of Sciences persistently to make appeals to the government concerning the transfer of the library. In 1958 it became an Academy Library and received the name State Public Scientific and Technical Library of the Siberian division of the Academy of Sciences of the USSR.[20] Thus the Academy received a third central library and a fourth library centre.

The significance of this act, from the point of view of state interests, is difficult to assess. The scientific research institutions of the Siberian division, with their colossal demands for scientific books and bibliographies, acquired a composite library. Its gigantic and well selected stock was transferred to an area where the library network had previously been extremely weak in comparison with Moscow.

The history of the state public scientific and technical library of the Siberian division is concerned with the preparation and transfer of stocks to Novosibirsk, with the planning and construction of special buildings, development of the most rational structure for the library, the scope of its acquisitions, the organisation of service to the academic and other scientific institutions and industrial undertakings in Siberia and the Far East. The library expanded the scope of acquisitions according to those divisions of natural sciences and the humanities which were poorly represented (biology, medicine, agriculture, geography, economics) in the stocks of the existing state scientific library. For several years after the transfer, the library of the Siberian division occupied the position of a central library of the Academy of Sciences of the USSR, taking upon itself all the work of the departmental libraries, including the guidance of staff, financing on a unified plan, methodological help, centralised acquisition and processing of literature, organisation of union catalogues and bibliographic service.

The library of the Siberian division is principally a new type of central Academy library. It is a public library for which it is equally important to give an active and comprehensive service to Academy institutions in Siberia and the Far East as well as a service to inquiries concerning industry, agriculture and culture, and to fulfil the function of a folklore centre. In 1966, a newly constructed building (for 10 million volumes) was acquired and the library was

88

in a favourable position to develop to the fullest extent all aspects of the work. But even up to then the activity of the library of the Siberian division has been closely connected with the national economic problems of the territory and with a striving towards satisfying inquiries from industry. The following signs are evidence of this fact: the predominance of engineers from Novosibirsk enterprises among the total number of readers and the subjects of bibliographies. The data on the growth of demand for bibliographic bulletins on current subjects shows in the increase in their circulation.

The problems of the further development of the Academy network in the last ten years have been more successfully solved than before both in Moscow and Leningrad. This is not limited to the increase in the number of libraries, but in addition the level of their work has improved and the network centres consistently accomplish distinctive coordinating and methodological functions.

	Circulation			
Bulletin	*1963*	*1964*	*1965*	*1966*
Soils of Siberia and the Far East	—	210	220	350
Vegetation and plant resources	165	210	220	450
Economics and organisation of industrial production	145	240	250	300

In 1960, the Fundamental Library of Social Sciences succeeded in centralising its labour consuming and expensive methods of processing literature. The results of centralisation of cataloguing are of use both for the organisation of the catalogues and the bibliographic card indexes.

At present, the Academy libraries persistently strive to overcome isolation, and to combine their efforts with those of libraries of other types and departments, for example in experiments in the issue of eighteen series of combined information lists of new foreign literature in all branches of the social sciences (history, economics, philosophy, history of literature and linguistics). In these lists, the Fundamental Library of Social Sciences uses the current entries for foreign literature from the Lenin State Library of the USSR, the All-Union State Library of Foreign Literature, the State Public

Historical Library of the Russian Soviet Federated Socialist Republic and also the departmental libraries of the Academy. Furthermore, six series on new Soviet literature concerning the social sciences were compiled. Thus the Fundamental Library appears in essence to be the centre of current social science information activity. The two other central libraries fulfil a similar function. These are the library of the Academy of Sciences, which is the centre for coordinating bibliographic activity in the field of natural sciences, and the library of the Siberian division for the coordination of work on local lore of Siberia and the Far East. The first significant step in this direction was the organisation in 1966 of a scientific conference on problems in the development of bibliographies of Siberia and the Far East by the Siberian Library Centre.[21]

The library network of the Academy of Sciences participates in and organises major inter-library undertakings. Groups of libraries of the Academy investigate a series of problems on the coordination of scientific research work with the Ministry of Culture (especially active in library and information problems), participate in many conferences on methods and also in the compilation of union catalogues of foreign literature in the Lenin State Library of the USSR, the All-Union State Library of Foreign Literature and the All-Union Institute of Scientific and Technical Information and the compilation of *Common rules for the description of printed works* and of a new library and bibliographic scheme of classification.

One of the prerequisites of library development in the last ten years has been the strengthening of attention by the guiding agents of the Academy of Sciences in the organisation of library affairs. In this, for example, many statutes of the Praesidium and Library Council (up to 1961 it was the Commission) are important, regulating international book exchange and the despatch of parcels of Academy publications to foreign scholars. The arrangements for the use of the manuscript collections in the Library of the Academy of Sciences in Leningrad, frequency of stocktaking and the rules for inter-library, international and national exchange of publications are other examples.

After thirteen years of irregular discussions the charters for the Library of the Academy of Sciences in Leningrad and the Fundamental Library of Social Sciences and also the position of the

90

libraries of the scientific institutes of the Academy were finally confirmed in 1958. Two years earlier the position of the libraries of branches of the Academy of Sciences of the USSR was also confirmed. In 1960, the charter of the state public scientific and technical library of the Siberian division of the Academy was accepted. Thus many years of work on the creation of statutes, regularising the organisational and legal foundations of the activities of the system of Academy libraries was concluded.

The resolution of the Praesidium of the Academy of Sciences of the USSR ' On the state and measures for improving the work of the libraries of the Academy of Sciences of the USSR ' (taken in September 1960) developed and consolidated, in conformity with the conditions of Academy libraries, the programmes and ideas of the resolution of the Central Committee of the Communist Party on library affairs (1959).[22]

REVIEW OF THE PRINCIPAL POINTS

Generalisation of the historical experience in the organisation of library service to the scientific institutions of the Academy of Sciences of the USSR leads to certain fundamental conclusions, enabling attention to be focused on the most essential achievements.

Absorbing into itself all the best that was in the past, the library network of the Academy of Sciences entered into a new, higher stage of its development after 1917. The important features of this period are: consolidation of the separate libraries, standardisation of their mutual ties and a change in the geography of the network (Moscow and Leningrad being the traditional and only library centres).

The years of Soviet rule have seen solutions to the basic problems of library development in the Academy of Sciences of the USSR, namely the creation of a unified system of interconnected and interacting central and departmental libraries, systematically and sharply limiting their functions in accordance with serving the academic institutions.

The departmental libraries, being branches of the central library and at the same time integral parts of the scientific institutions (branch, institute, laboratory), are committed to ensure daily and long-term ' problem ' subject service to their institutions, using for

91

the purpose the rich potentialities of the library centres, their stocks, catalogues and card indexes. The extent and character of the work of a departmental library are predetermined by the form and the scientific research plans of the institution.

The important significance of central libraries is their service to the Academy of Sciences. Together with this, in conformity with the Leninist principles of general accessibility of libraries, they must also show diversified help to the same wide circle of scientific, technical and engineering workers of non-Academy organisations. The library centres of the Academy each year increasingly fulfil the most consistent and successful missions of public libraries.

The administrative and methodological functions of the library centres are no less important. These include confirmation of the plans, accounts and regular schedules of the departmental libraries, the achievement of centralised acquisition and processing of literature, and methodological guidance.

It would be wrong to reduce the role of central libraries to one of central book storehouses or guidance centres for the network. Their task is to actively serve the needs of Soviet science as a whole through its branches, together with the departmental libraries of the Academy institutions. This enables the departmental libraries to concentrate their attention on effective service to the current inquiries of scientific institutions, being guided by the central library, actively furthering the fundamental bibliographical and general work of the central library, and adapting them to the specific needs of the institutes. For the central libraries, the fulfilment of their great work, demanding considerable time, corresponding book resources and reference tools as well as the high qualifications of the users, must be ensured as only these conditions can guarantee the systematic character and high level of such work.

Thus the close bond between the departmental and central libraries and the rational demarcation of their work in service to scientific work form the basis of their inter-relationship.

The organisation of service to readers from the beginnings of the branch arrangement is the indisputable achievement of the library network of the Academy of Sciences of the USSR. Such organisation makes it possible to regulate and control acquisition and mutual use of stocks of the academic libraries, helps the connection between central and departmental libraries, and ensures a high level and economic expediency of all library work. Centralisation in relation to foreign literature is especially effective, purchasing over a wide area though in small numbers. The proportion of foreign publications in the total stocks of the libraries of the Academy of Sciences of the USSR amounts to about forty percent and in the system of the Fundamental Library of Social Sciences to about fifty percent.

There is no doubt that without centralisation of acquisitions, cataloguing, compilation of bibliographies of the literature and, chiefly without regulating its mutual use, the problem of providing Soviet science with new information from foreign printed materials would not be solved.

In the branch system, rational definition of the boundaries of centralisation and decentralisation have primary significance. Centralised libraries provide for the labour-consuming work which it is economic to complete by a centralised system (acquisitions, cataloguing, the compilation of a union catalogue, collecting of requirements for inter-library exchange and book binding). Moreover the active role of departmental libraries in the choice of literature and direct library and bibliographic service to readers is not excluded. Unfortunately, the experience of the Academy of Sciences of the USSR in the organisation of the branch system of service to readers has not so far been studied very much. Meanwhile it might render invaluable help to those who are seriously preoccupied with problems of improving library affairs.

For the Academy of Sciences the result of the creation of a unified library stock in a rationally organised collection of printed material and manuscripts, accommodated in central and specialised libraries, is very important. Because of this success is achieved in avoiding the dissipation of resources, unnecessary duplication in acquisitions, burdening the stocks of literature in departmental libraries, as well as the withdrawal of unnecessary literature. The prerequisites are determined for a clear discrimination in the sphere of acquisitions between the central and departmental libraries, and also for library acquisitions plans to reflect the general methods of research work in the Academy of Sciences.

By unifying the stocks of every library it is possible, working with the whole of the academic stock, to secure such a service to readers whereby any book within the network, without regard to the location, is effectively available to the reader.

The advantages of the unity of the stocks are very distinct in the process of centralised acquisitions, distribution and redistribution of literature. Many years' experience has shown that only by this means is it possible to secure, on a large scale, the planned, co-ordinated and successive replenishment of the stocks of the library network. The development of centralised acquisitions may be carried out in any of the library centres of the Academy. The following table illustrates this sufficiently clearly.

Centralised acquisitions of Soviet literature by the libraries in the network

	Years					
	1939	*1944*	*1949*	*1954*	*1959*	*1964*
Number of libraries with centralised acquisitions	23	66	125	146	219	153
Total distributed literature (in thousand copies)	22·4	38·8	95·4	157·8	246·3	261·4

For undoubted success, it is necessary to carry out centralised processing of literature. The Academy of Sciences of the USSR first set about the centralised processing of current literature accessions at the beginning of the thirties, the Moscow branches followed in the second half of the thirties, the Fundamental Library of Social Sciences only solved this problem in 1960 and the Library of the Siberian division in 1964. With the introduction of centralised cataloguing into the library of the Siberian division, the important process of the development of centralised processing of literature over the entire system of libraries of the Academy of Sciences of the USSR was completed.

In arranging the rich book collections, accumulated over two and a half centuries, the libraries of the Academy of Sciences did much to organise the rational and effective use of these stocks and to achieve their maximum mobility. Through the solution of these problems, the following processes were facilitated: the centralisation of information on literature, the revealing of the contents of the combined stock through union catalogues and card indexes, the systematic organisation of exhibitions on specific subjects and information, the transfer of a considerable number of books for prolonged periods from the stocks of the central libraries to the departmental libraries,[23] various types of transfer, the organisation of inter-library loans and the introduction of copying facilities. The libraries of the Academy of Sciences of the USSR, especially the departmental libraries, even though not very effectively, used their valuable stocks for service to readers in institutions and divisions outside the Academy. Only a small fraction of the publications from the stocks of the Academy libraries (originals or copies) were destined for inter-library exchange with libraries of other departments.

These were important results gained during the fifty years of complex development of the libraries of the Academy of Sciences of the USSR. Many forms and methods of work, which now show growth and unification were produced in heated discussions. As long as ten years ago librarians regarded sceptically different forms of reprography. Now the library network of the Academy of Sciences has a considerable collection of reproduced materials (more than 50 thousand microfilms alone) and papers are reproduced from foreign journals for inter-library exchange and the most valuable foreign reference books and monographs are copied for the replenishment of stocks. A very promising innovation by the library of the Siberian division is the reproduction of required current foreign journals distributed by the central libraries.

In order to assess, according to merit, the path taken by the library network of the Academy in fifty years, it is advisable to make comparisons. Before the October Revolution, the book stocks of the central and fifteen departmental libraries slightly exceeded 2 million volumes. At the present time the library stocks of the Academy are reckoned at more than 52 million copies of scientific literature, of which almost forty percent consists of foreign material. Three central libraries and about 250 departmental libraries of scientific research institutes,[24] 170 mobile libraries and thirty distribution points for literature now serve the Academy of Sciences.

Information concerning the total number of readers in the Academy libraries in 1917 is not available but it is known that the number of regular readers in the Library of the Academy of

Sciences, for example, amounted to 780, and in the library of the Zoological Institute it amounted to 78. The former annually now serves more than 15 thousand and the latter 600-650 readers. As a whole the Academy libraries annually serve about 200 thousand scientific workers and supplies them with more than 25 million copies of publications. In the libraries of the Academy of Sciences of the USSR there is high book provision (260 copies per reader) and record readership (average for the network of libraries—138 issues per reader, and in some departmental libraries serving the humanities it reaches 600-700 copies).

According to the quantity and nature of bibliographic literature it is possible to judge not only the activities of the library, but also the level and the maturity of its science. If the bibliographic production of the Academy libraries is assessed from this point of view, then it is possible to affirm with good reason that it upholds the honour of Soviet science.

Even in the pre-revolution period there was a far from insignificant amount of interesting bibliographic work, but never did bibliography attain such a comprehensive character as it does now, on the eve of the fiftieth anniversary of Soviet rule. The distinguishing characteristic of the bibliographic activity of the Academy libraries has been the creation of a steady system of diverse bibliographic publications for the assistance of science. These included such media as information bulletins, retrospective branch indexes, subject bibliographies—all of which were regularly published in journals (*Uspekhi fizicheskikh nauk, Izvestiya Akademii nauk SSSR, Vestnik Akademii nauk SSSR, Prikladnaya matematika i mekhanika* and others), synopses, critical reviews of scientific literature and annuals of the Academy. The libraries of the Academy of Sciences developed valuable and original methods for compiling bibliographic material.

In the decrees of the Twenty Third Congress of the Communist Party, the necessity for creating a highly effective system of scientific information corresponding to the growing demands of scholars, engineers, inventors in industry and workers in state organisations is stated. These instructions found embodiment in a government resolution on the state system of scientific and technical information.[25] In it, great attention was paid to the role and place of scientific libraries in the system of scientific and technical information. It imposes high responsibility on the libraries of the Academy of Sciences of the USSR having indisputable achievements in information work. By the resolution of the government, responsibility for the production of bibliographic reference and survey information on world scientific and technical literature in the field of natural and technical sciences is entrusted to the Academy of Sciences of the USSR.

The Academy libraries obviously had to give up some traditional library forms of work and more actively introduce methods of information service to scientific workers in order to effectively disseminate information relevant to scientific research.

The products of information work would undoubtedly be enriched if the Academy libraries made more consistent and systematic use of the various types of unpublished material (reports on scientific research work, reviews and deposited manuscripts) in bibliographical service, organise regular reproduction and distribution of informational materials, effectively manage to mechanise and automate information services, and build up storehouses of information.

It should be understood that it is impossible to be limited by the above measures. Nevertheless they may help the library network of the Academy of Sciences of the USSR to be included in the state system of scientific and technical information.

Important historical, political, socialistic and economic causes assisted the establishment and development of the network of libraries of the Academy of Sciences of the USSR, promoting it to a level comparable with science libraries in other parts of the world. From the collections of literature in the rooms of individual scholars to the planned and organised system of research libraries, stretching effectively over the vast territories of the USSR—such is the historic path of the library network of the Academy of Sciences of the USSR, a vital part of the Soviet library system and the system of information service.

At the present time the attention of all Academy libraries is concentrated on raising the level of work in the light of the decree of the twenty third Congress of the Communist Party and the resolution of the Central Committee of the Party to meet the fiftieth anniversary of the Great October Revolution.

1 V D Bonch-Bruevich: (V I Lenin and the Library of the Academy of Sciences) *Novyi mir,* 1945 (8), page 101.

2 There is a considerable amount of literature on the academy libraries in the pre-revolutionary period, *see*: *Biblioteka Akademii nauk SSSR* (The Library of the Academy of Sciences) 1714-1964. Bibliographic index compiled by E P Faidel and others, edited by M S Filippov, page 308. Leningrad, Academy of Sciences Library, 1944.

3 G A Knyazev and A V Kol'tsov: *Kratkii ocherk istorii Akademii auk SSSR* (Short outline of the history of the Academy of Sciences USSR), third edition, page 93. Moscow, Nauka, 1964.

4 *Otchet o deyatel'nosti Akademii nauk SSSR za 1925* (Report on the activity of the Academy of Sciences USSR for 1925), page 37. Leningrad, 1926: *Akademiya nauk SSSR za desyat let 1917-1927* (The Academy of Sciences USSR during the decade 1917-1927), page 199. Leningrad, 1927.

5 *Otchet o deyatel'nosti Akademii nauk SSSR za 1927* (Report on the activity of the Academy of Sciences USSR for 1927), pages 45-46. Leningrad, 1928.

6 *Akademiya nauk SSSR za desyat let 1917-1927* (The Academy of Sciences USSR during the decade 1917-1927), pages 198-199. Leningrad, 1927.

7 (Plan of the main proposals for the organisation of library affairs in the Academy of Sciences of the USSR Leningrad, 1928) *Arkhiv AN SSSR* 158 2 349; *see also* the explanatory note to the plan in this reference.

8 V Uspenskii: (Three-year review and outlook of the work of the Library of the Akademy of Sciences) *Vestnik, Akademii nauk SSSR,* 1933 (6), pages 8-9.

9 After the amalgamation of the libraries of the Academy of Sciences and the Communist Academy in 1936, all the Moscow libraries of the Academy came into the library network of the Academy of Sciences of the USSR in 1936.

10 (The protocol of the meeting of the directorate of the Library of the Academy of Sciences with the heads of divisions from thirteen centres, 1934) *Arkhiv AN SSSR* 158 3 502; (Outline of special instructions on the guidance of the departmental libraries in the

Moscow network of the Academy of Sciences of the USSR and on the organisation of the temporary station of the Library of the Academy of Sciences in Moscow. Report of the Permanent Secretary of the Academy of Sciences of the USSR) *Arkhiv AN SSSR* 158 3 539.

11 *Biblioteka kommunisticheskoi akademii, ee organizatsiya i deyatel'nost 1918-1928* (The library of the Communist Academy, its organisation and activity 1918-1928), page 24. Moscow, 1928.

12 (Report of the Commission of Academician I V Grebenshchikov) Summary 1-3, *Arkhiv Biblioteki Akademii nauk SSSR,* 1936-7.

13 There is extensive literature covering the wartime period of library work in the Academy. For example *see: Istoriya Biblioteki Akademii nauk SSSR* (History of the Academy of Sciences USSR Library), volume 1, pages 427-461. Moscow-Leningrad, 1964; K I Shafranovskii: (The Library of the Academy of Sciences in Leningrad, 1941-1945) *Bibliotekar,* 1946 (4), pages 29-31; G Ya Snimshchikova: (The year of the blockade) in *Devyat'sot dnei* (Nine hundred days), second edition, pages 358-361. Leningrad, 1962.

14 V I Abramova: (The sixth conference of the heads of libraries of branches and other outlying institutions of the Academy of Sciences of the USSR) *Bibliotechno-bibliograficheskaya informatsiya bibliotek Akademii nauk SSSR i Akademii nauk soyuznykh respublik,* 1960 (28), pages 1-4; and also the review in the same journal, pages 165-202.

15 The bibliography named first in the text was published in the USSR from 1918 to 1960; part 1 1918-1945, Moscow, AN SSSR, 1963, 342 pages; the second bibliography was published in the USSR from 1918-1962, Moscow, Nauka, 1965, 276 pages.

16 (On the work of the network sector of departmental libraries of the Academy of Sciences of the USSR. Resolution of the Praesidium of the Academy of Sciences of the USSR, 6 February 1951) *Arkhiv, Sektor seti*; (On the subordination of the libraries of the institutes of the divisions of the social sciences in Moscow to the fundamental library of Social Sciences. Resolution of the Praesidium of the Academy of Sciences of the USSR, 14 December 1951) *Arkhiv, Fundamentalnaya biblioteka*; (On the work and condition of the staffs of the Library of the Academy of Sciences of the USSR.

Resolution of the Praesidium of the Academy of Sciences of the USSR, 10 March 1950) *Arkhiv, Fundamentalnaya biblioteka.*

17 (The organisation of the Eastern division of the Library of the Academy of Sciences of the USSR. Resolution of the Praesidium of the Academy of Sciences of the USSR, 17 August 1956, No 440) *Arkhiv, Bibliotechnyi Sovet.*

18 (On the transfer of the Eastern division of the Library of the Academy of Sciences of the USSR into the structure of the state public scientific and technical library of the Siberian Division of the Academy of Sciences of the USSR. Resolution of the Praesidium of the Academy of Sciences of the USSR, 19 August 1960, No 815) *Arkhiv, Bibliotechnyi Sovet.*

19 See: *Gosudarstvennaya nauchnaya biblioteka. K sorokaletiyu so dnya osnovaniya (1918-1958). Sbornik statei* (State scientific library. On the fortieth anniversary of its foundation 1918-1958. Collected papers). Moscow, 1959, 234 pages.

20 (Concerning the organisation of the state public scientific and technical library attached to the Siberian division of the Academy of Sciences of the USSR at Novosibirsk and of the state public scientific and technical library attached to the State Scientific and Technical Committee of the Council of Ministers of the USSR at Moscow. Resolution of the Council of Ministers of the USSR, 17 October 1958) *Sobranie postanovlenii pravitel'stva SSSR* (Collected resolutions of the Government of the USSR), no 17, page 136. Moscow, 1958.

21 *Postanovleniya nauchnoi konferentsii—problemy razvitiya bibliografii Sibiri i Dal'nego Vostoka* (Resolutions of the scientific conference—problems of the development of a bibliography of Siberia and the Far East), Novosibirsk, 5-8 October 1966. 12 pages.

22 (On the state and measures for improving library affairs in the country. Resolution of the Central Committee of the Communist Party of the Soviet Union. 22 September 1959) *Voprosy ideologicheskoi raboty* (Problems of ideological work), pages 209-215. Moscow, 1961.

23 For example, annually some 50 thousand copies of foreign literature for long term use are transferred to the Fundamental Library of the Social Sciences.

100

24 The number of libraries has changed at various periods over the last fifty years. Many of these supplemented the library systems of other departments (the industrial ministries and the academies of sciences in the Union republics).

25 *Sobranie postanovlenii pravitel'stva SSSR* (Collected resolutions of the government of the USSR), no 25, page 220. Moscow, 1966.

VI LIBRARY AFFAIRS IN THE USSR—STATISTICS
by M M POLUBOYARINOV[1]

During the course of socialist development in our country, the pattern of national culture was truly moulded. The spread of national education indicates above all the scale and extent of the cultural revolution. From 1920 to 1940 up to 60 million people were taught to read and write in the USSR, this demand for knowledge by the workers being unprecedented in history.

Until the October Revolution four out of every five children of school age had no chance of an education. In the directives of the five year plan for the development of the national economy in 1966-1970, provision is made to virtually complete, by the end of this period, the transfer to universal secondary education both in the towns and in the country.

From 1918-1966 higher educational establishments trained seven million specialists. Eleven million persons received training in technical schools and special secondary schools, and in 1966 more than 73 million people were involved in all forms of training (including training and higher qualifications directly from industry and from set courses) within the Soviet Union. This indicates that every third citizen (not counting children up to school age) is receiving an education. In schools providing general education alone in the 1966/1967 school year, more than 48 million persons were taught—a five hundred percent increase over 1914.

In 1913 the output of books totalled less than 100 million and that of papers three million copies. In the USSR from 1918-1966, more than two million books and brochures were published, the total number of copies exceeding 31 thousand million. In 1966 by comparison with 1913, the number of copies of books published increased 13 times and newspapers 34 times. At present for every 100 people 541 copies of books and 47 copies of newspapers (in tzarist Russia 62 and 2 respectively) are issued.

From the first days of Soviet rule library affairs acquired the character of a state system. Lenin repeatedly emphasised that a successful solution to the problem of economic, political and cultural development was impossible without the active promotion of books. Today it is possible to point out that Lenin's directions regarding the increased availability of books to the population are, to a considerable extent, fulfilled. In the vast territory of the Soviet state, a wide network of libraries of different types has been created, possessing vast and valuable book resources.

TABLE 1 : *Increase in the number of libraries and their stocks (at the beginning of the year)*

	1914	1935	1941	1965
Libraries (in thousands)	75	116	277	367
Stocks (books and periodicals in millions)	46	299	527	2,331

On the eve of the first world war there were 76 thousand libraries of all types in Russia and their total book stock reached just 46 million copies. On an average each library had about 600 books, pamphlets and periodicals. In the Tambov province, for example, one library had 304 books, and in the Vologda province 469. Scientific and research libraries (of which there were less than 3 thousand) contained approximately 14 million items.

In 1965, as can be seen, there is no comparison with 1914, the number of libraries having increased almost five times and their book stocks fifty one times. Finally, the modern library as a registered unit is not comparable with the library in tzarist Russia. Among the 76 thousand pre-revolutionary libraries, very small ones, mainly in parish schools, predominated, their stocks being insignificantly small. Therefore the figures in TABLE 1 give only an approximate representation of the growth of the number of libraries and of their stocks. The structure of the library network was changed in relation to the needs of the developing national economy, science and culture.

In 1914, the major libraries of Russia comprised less than twenty percent of all the libraries, and in 1965 almost thirty five percent. Now these libraries have universally available book stocks, satisfying the most varied inquiries for literature. The proportion of the book stocks in libraries of this type now amounts to forty three percent as compared to twenty one percent in 1921.

The proportion of school libraries was considerably reduced from seventy eight percent in 1914 (including libraries of parish schools) to fifty two percent in 1965, notwithstanding the great overall growth in their numbers.

An important role in satisfying inquiries on science, industry and culture is at the present time played by scientific and research libraries, which help in the solution of problems of scientific and technical progress and in increasing the scientific and industrial qualifications of scientific workers and specialists. These libraries contain almost half the stocks of all the libraries in the country.

During the years of Soviet rule libraries were created in industrial undertakings, in scientific institutions and higher educational establishments. Of the total number of scientific and technical libraries, 13 thousand, or more than a quarter, consist of libraries of industrial undertakings, a fifth consists of libraries serving workers in central and local government organisations, and nine percent consists of libraries of scientific institutions and planning organisations. A third of the book stocks of research libraries is concentrated in the libraries of scientific institutions and planning organisations and more than a fifth is concentrated in the libraries of higher educational institutions.

The number of libraries of higher educational establishments and the scientific institutions is relatively small and the proportion of them in the total number of scientific, technical and research libraries is little more than ten percent. However, it must be taken into consideration that in this group there are the great scientific, technical and reference libraries which are essentially independent scientific institutions.

In the Soviet Union technical libraries are vital parts of industrial concerns, and the stocks of technical libraries represent considerable book resources. The libraries of industrial concerns contain 111 million copies of books and periodicals.

With the development of secondary research education, libraries began to be formed by technical institutes, in which are found nine percent of the book stock of the research libraries. Students in technical schools and other establishments of professional and technical education are also well provided with libraries. The decrease in the number of technical and research libraries of different forms in the period from 1961 to 1965 is connected chiefly with reorganisation and the amalgamation of small libraries.

TABLE 2: *Distribution of scientific, technical and research libraries according to form and subordination*

Libraries	Number of libraries (thousands)		Book stocks (millions)	
	1961	1965	1961	1965
Libraries of central and local organisations and institutions	10·1	10·4	90	85
Scientific institutions and planning organisations	3·9	4·6	211	332
Higher education establishments	0·8	0·8	172	219
Technical schools and other secondary special educational establishments	3·2	3·7	69	94
Establishments for professional and technical education	3·9	5·1	28	42
Undertakings in industry, construction and transport	13·4	13·2	82	111
Hospitals, sanitoria and other medical institutions	14·6	13·0	116	112
Total	49·9	50·8	768	995

At the same time it is necessary to mention the rapid increase in stocks in all types of libraries (TABLE 3). The stocks of scientific libraries and libraries in scientific research institutions increased especially rapidly. Annually libraries (not counting the school libraries) as a whole acquired about 200 million books, pamphlets and periodicals. According to the State budget, more than 200 million roubles were spent in a year on the contents of libraries alone. To this it is necessary to add the expenditure on libraries of trade union organisations and collective farms.

Educational establishments, technical institutes, planning and construction organisations have comparatively large libraries; 162 libraries contain more than half a million industrial publications in their stocks.

105

TABLE 3: *Size of library stocks (in percentages)*

Book stocks	Independent public libraries of cultural organizations		Technical and research libraries	
	1961	*1965*	*1961*	*1965*
up to 1,000	1	1	30	27
from 1,001 to 6,000	55	49	32	32
from 6,001 to 10,000	25	30	12	12
over 10,000	19	20	26	29

In the last thirty years, the stock of the Lenin State Library has increased by 14 million copies, or by 2·5 times; the Saltykov-Schedrin State Public Library by 7 millions, or doubled; the Gorky Science Library by more than 5 million copies, or by almost eight times; the all-Union State Library of Foreign Literature by 3·1 millions, or by twelve times; the Central Scientific and Technical Library of the Ministry of Communication by 1·6 million copies, or by eight times; the Central Scientific and Agricultural Library of the all-Union Academy of Agricultural Sciences by more than 1·3 million, or by four times. In many Union republics the stocks of the leading libraries increased from one to two hundred times.

Following the directions of Lenin, national educational organisations carried out a considerable reorganisation of the library network. But it is obvious that the colossal work confronting the young Soviet republic could not be expressed in library affairs: the library network sometimes increased and sometimes decreased. Even during the first year of the period of library reconstruction the network was four thousand times greater than in tzarist Russia on the eve of the first world war. The book stocks in 1924, by comparison with 1913, had increased by more than five times and reached 52 million copies. The library network after 1925 increased with great speed during the period of industrialisation of the country and the collectivisation of farming. During 1927 alone, the increase in libraries amounted to about 5 thousand, or twenty two percent, and the book stock increased by 8 million copies. The Party and the government took measures to open libraries in the villages and to replenish their book stocks, the principles of regular geographic distribution of libraries being considered more and more.

TABLE 4: *Development of the network of public libraries and the increase in their stocks during the first ten years of Soviet rule*

	Totals in towns and country districts		In towns		In country districts	
Year	Number of libraries	Stock (in thousands)	Number of libraries	Stock (in thousands)	Number of libraries	Stock (in thousands)
1913	13,876	9,442	2,575	4,975	11,301	4,467
1921	17,725	45,758	2,976	34,534	14,749	11,224
1922	16,604	46,257	6,057	34,871	10,547	11,386
1923	16,256	47,343	4,550	35,937	11,706	11,406
1924	17,762	51,848	4,929	37,376	12,833	14,472
1925	20,491	54,389	4,490	35,634	16,001	18,755
1926	21,703	61,482	4,462	41,190	17,241	20,292
1927	26,492	69,202	7,538	43,521	18,954	25,681

NOTE: Some lowering in the figures for 1922-1926 is explained by a reduction in the state allocation during the period of the new economic policy and the number of libraries closed by it.

The library network rapidly increased, not only in the centre of the country, but also in the farthest corners of tzarist Russia where, up to the establishment of Soviet rule, there had been few libraries, and those possessed small and biased stocks (*see* TABLE 5).

Until the revolution, the people of Russia were very poorly supplied with books. By 1913, in 13,876 public libraries, there were only 9,442 thousand books and periodicals, each library had on average 680 items; there being six items for every inhabitant. Thus the so-called national publications consisted mainly of pamphlets, predominantly of a religious, moral, monarchist and chauvinistic character. Very few good books were produced for the public and these were rarely available in libraries.

Let us examine how the network of public libraries developed during the years of the first five year plan. The number of libraries was considerably increased during the first, second and subsequent years. Some stabilisation of the network and even a slight fall in the number of libraries were observed in 1930-1931. This is explained by the cessation of their activities or their amalgamation with small libraries created earlier. In accordance with the five year plan libraries increased by more than six thousand, or by a quarter, and the book stocks increased by 27 million copies or by almost a third. Annually the average increase in the library stocks amounted to 4 million copies. The stocks of urban libraries grew more rapidly having an incomparably better base on which to build. In 1932, on average, a town library contained rather more than a thousand items. The number of libraries in rural areas during the five year plan increased by twenty six percent, and in the towns by twenty percent.

TABLE 5 : *Distribution of public libraries in 1913 in the territories of the present Union republics*

	Number of libraries	Stock (in thousands)	Number of books and periodicals on an average per 100 inhabitants	In each library
Russian Soviet Federated Socialist Republic	9,342	6,698	7	717
Ukrainian SSR	3,153	1,917	5	608
Belorussian SSR	851	423	6	497
Uzbek SSR	—	—	—	—
Kazakh SSR	139	98	2	705
Georgian SSR	25	18	1	720
Azerbaijan SSR	25	18	1	720
Lithuanian SSR	27	31	1	1,148
Moldavian SSR	72	54	3	750
Latvian SSR	112	126	5	1,125
Kirghiz SSR	—	—	—	—
Tajik SSR	—	—	—	—
Armenian SSR	13	9	1	692
Turkmen SSR	—	—	—	—
Estonian SSR	117	50	5	427

It is important to mention that as early as the tenth anniversary of the Great October Revolution the library network was established in Central Asia, where there had been no libraries before the revolution. In the Uzbek SSR, for example, the number of libraries increased from 162 in 1927, to 609 in 1932, in the Tajik SSR from eleven to 119, in the Turkmen SSR from twenty six to 166 libraries. The book stocks also increased considerably.

TABLE 6: *Development of the network of public libraries during the years of the first five year plan*

Year	In towns and rural areas		In towns		In rural areas	
	Number of libraries	Stock (in thousands)	Number of libraries	Stock (in thousands)	Number of libraries	Stock (in thousands)
1927	26,492	69,202	7,538	43,521	18,954	25,681
1928	28,864	72,166	7,970	46,763	20,894	25,403
1929	29,949	79,636	8,964	54,113	20,985	25,518
1930	27,464	91,206	7,807	64,179	19,657	27,027
1931	27,737	90,399	8,546	59,582	19,191	30,958
1932	32,918	91,284	9,066	60,326	23,852	30,958

TABLE 7: *Development of the library network in the years of the first five year plan in the Union republics (up to November 1939)*

	1927		1932	
	Number of libraries	Stock (in thousands)	Number of libraries	Stock (in thousands)
Russian Soviet Federated Socialist Republic	16,940	48,576	18,143	60,352
Ukrainian SSR	8,702	16,556	10,492	22,638
Belorussian SSR	276	1,180	1,427	2,389
Uzbek SSR	162	312	609	1,370
Kazakh SSR	236	488	354	629
Georgian SSR	363	633	785	1,018
Azerbaijan SSR	114	1,017	167	1,757
Moldavian SSR	78	88	191	241
Kirghiz SSR	50	61	89	105
Tajik SSR	11	12	119	107
Armenian SSR	154	155	426	358
Turkmen SSR	36	123	116	325

In the second five year plan, libraries were opened in response to the development of more institutions of culture, industrial undertakings and agricultural cooperatives. The introduction of widespread compulsory elementary education demanded an expansion of the library network and an increase in the stocks of public libraries. The problems of libraries in reading guidance became more complicated by the provision of help to workers in self education. All this dictated the necessity for careful examination of the activities of libraries and of the scientific approach to them.

In conformity with the resolution of the Central Executive Committee of the USSR of 27 March 1934, ' On library affairs in the USSR ', for the first time in history a state census of libraries was carried out on a national scale. It was carried out by agents for state statistics together with agents for national education and trade union organisations. N K Krupskaya took an active part in the preparation and carrying out of the census, and the data obtained concerning the library network, its resources and the duties, as well as the number and composition of the library staffs, gave considerable help in improving book service to the population. In the USSR at the end of 1934, 116 thousand libraries of different types, with a book stock of about 300 million copies, could be counted. In comparison with the pre-revolution period, the book stocks of the libraries had increased 6·5 times.[2]

In 1933 and 1934, the number of public libraries increased by almost 18 thousand, or one and a half times, and their book stocks increased by 4 million copies.

For the seventeen years immediately after the Great October Revolution, the network of libraries took shape, enabling the requirements of all levels of the population to be satisfied, not only for artistic, social and political information, but also for scientific, technical, popular, educational, industrial and children's literature. Public libraries comprised the greatest proportion of the libraries (forty four percent) at that time. In addition there were a great number of research, scientific, technical, educational and reference libraries. In the library census, 104 thousand mobile libraries were registered of which more than 92 thousand belonged to public libraries. In 1934, only 55·2 thousand qualified librarians were counted, of which 34 thousand worked in public libraries.

After serious analysis of the data gained from the census, planning and executive organs carried out necessary work of organising the library network. This helped, in the years of the second five year plan, to solve a number of important problems connected with the creation of new libraries and the development of resources for the existing libraries. As a result, during the second five year plan alone, the number of libraries increased twofold or more, in the country areas increasing 2·4 times and in the towns 1·5 times. The book stocks grew by 35 million copies, or by more than a third : by 23 million copies (thirty nine percent) in urban libraries, and by 12 million copies (almost forty percent) in rural areas. In the four years after the all-Union library census alone, the book stock increased from 299 millions to 443 millions. Moreover the book stocks of the independent scientific libraries and the libraries of scientific research institutions increased by 11 million copies, or by a third, and those of the technical and special libraries of industrial undertakings, machine tractor stations and state farms by almost two times.

TABLE 8 : *Development of the network of public libraries in the years of the second five year plan*

	In towns and rural areas		In towns		In rural areas	
Year	Number of libraries	Stock (in thousands)	Number of libraries	Stock (in thousands)	Number of libraries	Stock (in thousands)
1932	32,918	91,284	9,066	60,326	23,852	30,958
1933	40,316	86,009	13,279	57,674	27,037	28,335
1934	50,870	94,884	14,514	68,524	36,356	26,360
1935	51,709	103,910	12,449	71,193	39,260	32,717
1936	55,887	116,386	12,638	79,100	43,249	37,286
1937	69,975	126,640	13,801	83,619	56,174	43,021

In the years of the third five year plan our country changed to universal seven year education and the number of secondary and higher educational institutions increased extensively. This was one of the causes for the continuous growth in the number of libraries, not only in towns but also in rural areas.

In the USSR, at the end of the prewar period in 1940, 277 libraries of all types were developed in which were more than 500 million books and journals. By comparison with 1934, the number of libraries of all kinds móre than doubled and their book stocks increased by 228 million copies, or by 1·8 times. It should be mentioned that in the third five year plan, the network of public libraries developed more uniformly. Annually the number of libraries increased by 8-9 thousand and their stocks by 20 million copies (*see* TABLE 9).

TABLE 9: *Development of the network of public libraries in the prewar years*

	In towns and rural areas		In towns		In rural areas	
Year	Number of libraries	Stock (in thousands)	Number of libraries	Stock (in thousands)	Number of libraries	Stock (in thousands)
1937	69,975	126,640	13,801	83,619	56,174	43,021
1938	77,775	147,573	15,952	98,377	61,823	49,196
1939	86,312	166,764	16,970	110,096	69,342	56,698
1940	95,401	184,767	18,454	120,593	76,947	64,174

By 1941, a stable library network had been set up, in every republic, region, territory and district, capable of providing books for a considerable proportion of the workers in towns and villages. The problem of creating public libraries in every district and rural soviet was successfully solved. In almost all districts, district libraries were developed, in every rural soviet some libraries (including those of collective farms) were also established. In the rural areas alone, 77 thousand public libraries, the book stocks of which reached 64 million copies, could be counted.

In 1941, the network of public libraries had rich stocks available: on an average there was a stock of two thousand copies of books and periodicals per library and moreover for each independent library of cultural organisations, there were 6·5 thousand books. Each rural library had two thousand books.

Following the German fascist invasion the work of the Soviet people was interrupted. During the war a great number of industrial undertakings, collective farms, schools, higher educational organisations, technical schools, hospitals (which had libraries), libraries and other cultural institutions were wrecked. Libraries in the affected districts suffered especially, being subject to temporary occupation by fascist troops. More than 100 million volumes were destroyed or plundered by fascists from the stocks of public libraries alone. The libraries of higher educational institutions lost more than 43 million copies of books during the war years.[3]

TABLE 10: *The spread of public libraries according to type and department under which they worked at the end of 1940*

Library	Number of libraries	Stock (in thousands)	Number of books and periodicals on average in each library
All public libraries including:	95,401	184,767	1,937
State	55,863	113,730	2,036
independent	14,881	96,532	6,487
republican (ASSR) territorial and regional	125	18,510	148,080
district and neighbourhood	3,683	33,332	9,050
town	1,221	18,027	14,764
rural	8,613	16,438	1,909
children's	1,239	10,225	8,253
in club establishments	40,982	17,198	420
Collective farm libraries	17,817	4,526	254
Trade union organisations	17,790	58,395	3,284
Of other departments and organisations	3,931	8,116	2,064

At the beginning of 1946 the number of public libraries in the country was half that in 1940, *ie* reduced by almost 58 thousand, and their book stocks by more than 76 million copies. The Soviet people rapidly managed to restore industry, agriculture and culture. Already by 1950 more than 350 thousand libraries of different types could be counted; an increase of 74 thousand over 1940. The stocks of all libraries in 1950 amounted to 714 million copies, which is 187 million more than the prewar library figure.

The state network was also restored at a very rapid rate. It almost doubled from 1946 to 1950 and the libraries of trade union organisations increased 2·6 times. The number of libraries in collective farms increased almost 1·9 times. The most marked increase in number was in the network of rural libraries (3·1 times) and in the children's libraries (2·6 times). In comparison with 1946, the book stocks as a whole were doubled by 1950, and the stocks of cultural organisations were increased 3·1 times.[4]

In the postwar five year plan, the network of libraries in all the Union republics was restored and expanded. The number of public libraries alone increased over the whole of the country by 2·6 times and their stocks were more than doubled. In the Lithuanian SSR, in this period, the number of libraries increased 7·4 times and their stocks increased 4·6 times; in the Ukrainian SSR the figures were 7·2 and five respectively, and in the Tajik SSR were 5·6 and three respectively.

In 1956, by comparison with 1950, the number of libraries of all types in the USSR increased by 43 thousand. The number of public libraries increased by 21 thousand, and the number of technical and research libraries increased by 15 thousand. The data of TABLE 11 shows that the library network of all types increased for the named period by twelve percent, and the book stocks were at least doubled (increased by 800 million copies), moreover the stocks of public libraries increased 2·7 times.

Comparison of the number of libraries and their book stocks which had developed in the USSR by 1956, with the comparative data for 1913, shows that the number of libraries increased 5·2 times and their stocks 3·3 times. The number of public libraries rose ten more times and their stocks sixty nine times. Technical and research libraries rose twenty four times and their stocks forty eight times. From 1951 up to 1956, the book stocks rose not only on account of newly organised library institutions but also to a considerable extent on account of the replenishment of stocks libraries created earlier. This process proceeded in all the Union republics, which TABLE 12 clearly shows. On the fortieth anniversary of the Great October Revolution, about 400 thousand different libraries with a

114

stock of more than one and a half thousand million copies of printed material could be counted.

For the purpose of further improvement in the activities of Soviet libraries, the Central Committee of the Communist Party took a resolution in 1959 ' On the state and measures for improving library affairs in the country ', in which important problems were covered connected with the arrangement of the network, acquisition of stocks and with improvement in the service of books to the people.

TABLE 11 : *Growth of the network of libraries of all types from 1951-1955*

	1950	1956	1956 (as a percentage of 1950)
Total number of libraries (thousands)	351	394	112
Books and periodicals in them (million copies)	714	1,510	211
Of the total number :			
Public libraries	123	144	117
and their books and periodicals	244	653	267
Libraries of general education schools and children's homes	180	187	103
and their books and periodicals	82	174	211
Technical and other research libraries	48	63	132
and their books and periodicals	388	683	176

Being guided by this resolution, cultural and trade union organisations combined some small libraries; obsolete literature was now excluded from library stocks and new libraries were organised where none existed previously. As a result of a number of measures and also in connection with the recontruction of the national economy, the number of libraries of all types was somewhat reduced. For example, in rural areas, an amalgamation of independent libraries with club libraries and of state libraries with collective farm libraries was carried out. At the same time although a considerable part of the obsolete stocks was discarded, the overall stocks were considerably increased. At the end of 1963, there were 354 thousand libraries of all types, in which could be counted more than two thousand million books and periodicals.

TABLE 12 : *Libraries of all types*

	1950		1956	
	Number of libraries	Stocks (in libraries	Number of thousands)	Stocks (in thousands)
USSR	351,137	713,936	394,236	1,509,713
Russian Soviet Feder-ated Socialist Republic	205,550	480,584	223,309	922,182
Ukrainian SSR	77,149	126,722	80,156	295,684
Belorussian SSR	15,675	14,161	21,453	44,687
Uzbek SSR	4,978	11,526	7,998	33,701
Kasakh SSR	10,335	14,403	15,053	39,532
Georgian SSR	5,852	13,655	7,797	32,018
Azerbaijan SSR	4,737	10,327	5,919	21,387
Lithuanian SSR	7,123	5,474	8,571	23,847
Moldavian SSR	3,833	4,260	4,402	15,838
Latvian SSR	4,539	9,613	5,265	22,737
Kirghiz SSR	1,954	3,245	2,721	8,005
Tajik SSR	1,701	3,130	2,270	8,463
Armenian SSR	2,631	6,519	2,803	15,273
Turkmen SSR	1,908	3,629	2,717	9,816
Estonian SSR	3,172	6,688	3,802	16,543

In the USSR in 1963, 126 thousand public libraries were in operation, which was nine times greater than the total in tzarist Russia in 1913. Their book stocks, by comparison with the pre-revolutionary period had increased 100 times, and at the beginning of 1964 had reached 950 million copies (approximately half included the stocks of rural libraries).

Comparison of the data for 1963 and 1940 shows that the number of libraries increased by a third, and the stocks by five times, moreover in towns library stocks increased by four times and in rural areas by seven times. It should be mentioned that after the resolution of the Central Committee of the Communist Party of the Soviet Union of 1959, the number of public libraries decreased slightly (in 1963, by comparison with 1958, a decrease of eight percent), and on the other hand the book stocks increased by 196

116

million copies, or seventeen percent (with a decrease in the network
of rural libraries of sixteen percent). TABLE 13 helps to trace the
change in the network of public libraries from 1959-1963.

TABLE 13: *Public libraries in 1958-1963*

	In towns and rural areas		In towns		In rural areas	
Year	Number of libraries (*thousands*)	Stock (*in millions*)	Number of libraries (*thousands*)	Stock (*in millions*)	Number of libraries (*thousands*)	Stock (*in millions*)
1958	138	753	29	369	109	384
1959	138	803	33	404	105	399
1960	136	845	35	432	101	413
1961	134	897	35	462	99	435
1962	133	921	36	479	97	442
1963	126	949	35	499	91	450

On the eve of the fiftieth anniversary of the Great October
Revolution about 370 thousand libraries of different types are
established, the book stocks of which exceeded 2·3 thousand million
copies. In comparison with the pre-revolutionary period the stocks
of libraries have increased fifty one times.

A network of state, regional, republic, town district and rural
libraries and also libraries of collective farms and trade unions
now functions in every republic.

TABLE 14: *Public libraries of various types and belonging to various
departments*

	1950		1965	
	Number of libraries	Stock (*in thousands*)	Number of libraries	Stock (*in thousands*)
USSR				
All public libraries	123,077	244,243	127,334	1,052,329
Libraries of cultural organisations	81,870	168,765	84,129	789,596
These include: republican (ASSR), territorial & regional	143	23,595	141	66,923

TABLE 14 (*continued*)

	1950		1965	
	Number of libraries	*Stock (in thousands)*	*Number of libraries*	*Stock (in thousands)*
district and neigh-bourhood	4,356	38,139	3,935	90,291
town	1,888	25,414	5,047	135,382
independent rural	17,265	33,690	59,195	355,677
independent children's	2,160	16,855	4,972	113,277
in club establish-ments	56,058	31,072	10,839	28,046
Libraries of collective farms	22,183	6,397	5,759	11,620
Libraries of trade union organisations	13,111	52,381	27,606	216,440
Libraries of other departments and organisations	5,913	16,700	3,364	27,138
RSFSR (Russian Soviet Federated Socialist Republic)				
All public libraries	59,407	159,192	63,065	602,125
Libraries of cultural organisations	41,844	106,403	40,527	438,610
These include: republican (ASSR), territorial & regional	62	16,931	76	49,768
district & neigh-bourhood	2,540	25,984	2,598	57,964
town	1,064	16,539	2,568	74,146
independent rural	8,993	21,647	30,094	176,714
independent children's	1,050	10,262	2,754	66,328

118

TABLE 14 (*continued*)

| | *1950* | | *1965* | |
	Number of libraries	Stock (in thousands)	Number of libraries	Stock (in thousands)
in club establishments	28,135	15,040	2,437	3,690
Libraries of collective farms	6,764	1,803	1,012	2,247
Libraries of trade union organisations	7,327	38,236	15,848	145,546
Libraries of other departments and organisations	3,472	12,750	1,643	10,984
Ukrainian SSR				
All public libraries	34,913	42,945	29,235	228,722
Libraries of cultural organisations	18,947	2,912	18,817	173,739
These include:				
republican (ASSR), territorial & regional	25	3,798	24	10,223
district & neighbourhood	790	6,003	539	14,812
town	227	2,964	1,039	25,395
independent rural	3,661	5,581	14,103	91,011
independent children's	613	4,187	924	24,602
in club establishments	13,631	6,599	2,188	7,696
Libraries of collective farms	10,862	3,025	1,672	2,562
Libraries of trade union organisations	3,206	8,559	6,650	42,195
Libraries of other departments and organisations	1,898	2,229	991	8,960

119

TABLE 14 (*continued*)

	1950		1965	
	Number of libraries	*Stock (in thousands)*	*Number of libraries*	*Stock (in thousands)*
Belorussian SSR				
All public libraries	4,847	6,543	7,280	42,213
Libraries of cultural organisations	3,597	5,427	5,370	35,408
These include:				
republican (ASSR), territorial & regional	12	1,125	6	1,709
district & neighbourhood	175	1,117	100	2,774
town	57	450	150	5,036
independent rural	437	403	1,919	12,247
independent children's	48	226	191	4,255
in club establishments	2,868	2,106	3,004	9,387
Libraries of collective farms	828	106	492	461
Libraries of trade union organisations	264	615	1,028	4,516
Libraries of other departments and organisations	158	395	189	1,493
Uzbek SSR				
All public libraries	1,527	3,333	4,893	21,682
Libraries of cultural organisations	750	2,424	2,762	15,653
These include:				
republican (ASSR), territorial & regional	10	596	10	1,322

TABLE 14 (*continued*)

	1950		1965	
	Number of libraries	*Stock (in thousands)*	*Number of libraries*	*Stock (in thousands)*
district & neigh-bourhood	136	666	140	2,654
town	61	481	129	2,842
independent rural	360	399	1,182	4,216
independent children's	52	167	192	3,077
in club establish-ments	131	115	1,109	1,542
Libraries of collective farms	568	177	1,176	1,640
Libraries of trade union organisations	209	732	731	3,623
Libraries of other departments and organisations	—	—	40	601
Kazakh SSR				
All public libraries	4,335	6,329	6,644	38,495
Libraries of cultural organisations	3,467	4,988	4,720	29,773
These include: republican (ASSR), territorial & regional	16	701	16	2,689
district & neigh-bourhood	202	1,225	188	3,317
town	76	602	319	4,806
independent rural	408	514	3,663	15,276
independent children's	87	342	295	3,245
in club establish-ments	2,678	1,604	239	440

TABLE 14 (*continued*)

	1950		*1965*	
	Number of libraries	*Stock (in thousands)*	*Number of libraries*	*Stock (in thousands)*
Libraries of collective farms	324	109	70	181
Libraries of trade union organisations	502	1,075	1,205	7,214
Libraries of other departments and organisations	42	157	63	734
Georgian SSR				
All public libraries	2,183	5,097	3,083	18,327
Libraries of cultural organisations	1,875	3,681	2,504	15,298
These include :				
republican (ASSR), territorial & regional	3	164	3	506
district & neighbourhood	49	283	66	1,580
town	97	901	127	2,955
independent rural	209	321	1,032	4,662
independent children's	55	295	111	2,096
in club establishments	1,462	1,717	1,165	3,499
Libraries of collective farms	78	95	167	545
Libraries of trade union organisations	123	725	339	2,204
Libraries of other departments and organisations	107	596	12	130

TABLE 14 (*continued*)

	1950		*1965*	
	Number of libraries	*Stock (in thousands)*	*Number of libraries*	*Stock (in thousands)*
Azerbaijan SSR				
All public libraries	2,290	4,203	2,412	18,459
Libraries of cultural organisations	1,471	2,912	1,914	15,625
These include:				
republican (ASSR), territorial & regional	2	44	2	211
district & neighbourhood	71	489	60	1,681
town	53	973	105	3,388
independent rural	350	430	1,576	8,177
independent children's	54	431	88	1,870
in club establishments	941	545	83	298
Libraries of collective farms	706	393	224	547
Libraries of trade union organisations	105	873	187	1,982
Libraries of other departments and organisations	8	25	65	277
Lithuanian SSR				
All public libraries	3,726	2,609	2,224	16,998
Libraries of cultural organisations	3,632	2,419	1,797	13,740
These include:				
republican (ASSR), territorial & regional	4	44	—	—

TABLE 14 (*continued*)

	1950		1965	
	Number of libraries	*Stock (in thousands)*	*Number of libraries*	*Stock (in thousands)*
district & neigh-bourhood	50	302	44	928
town	48	266	108	2,378
independent rural	455	841	1,589	9,907
independent children's	10	36	56	527
in club establish-ments	3,065	930	—	—
Libraries of collective farms	1	6	5	16
Libraries of trade union organisations	73	170	232	1,294
Libraries of other departments and organisations	20	14	151	1,902
Moldavian SSR				
All public libraries	1,654	2,110	1,651	13,709
Libraries of cultural organisations	1,526	1,981	1,122	10,285
These include :				
district & neigh-bourhood	60	403	24	667
town	9	204	67	2,007
independent rural	299	412	874	5,831
independent children's	50	317	43	1,524
in club establish-ments	1,108	645	114	256
Libraries of collective farms	18	5	260	1,753
Libraries of trade union organisations	79	95	196	1,036

TABLE 14 (*continued*)

	1950		1965	
	Number of libraries	*Stock (in thousands)*	*Number of libraries*	*Stock (in thousands)*
Libraries of other departments and organisations	31	29	22	571
Latvian SSR				
All public libraries	2,343	2,863	1,619	13,570
Libraries of cultural organisations	769	2,121	902	9,736
These include:				
district & neighbourhood	44	363	21	668
town	63	701	111	3,428
independent rural	652	1,008	683	4,112
independent children's	10	49	87	1,528
in club establishments	—	—	—	—
Libraries of collective farms	912	304	145	548
Libraries of trade union organisations	662	438	491	2,760
Libraries of other departments and organisations	—	—	63	477
Kirghiz SSR				
All public libraries	1,004	1,233	1,280	8,486
Libraries of cultural organisations	790	931	751	6,274
These include:				
republican (ASSR), territorial & regional	6	110	1	182

TABLE 14 (*continued*)

	1950		1965	
	Number of libraries	*Stock (in thousands)*	*Number of libraries*	*Stock (in thousands)*
district & neighbourhood	62	264	29	608
town	15	108	41	1,617
independent rural	161	134	589	2,498
independent children's	17	92	48	1,302
in club establishments	529	223	43	67
Libraries of collective farms	85	21	249	526
Libraries of trade union organisations	61	117	128	985
Libraries of other departments and organisations	68	164	40	652
Tajik SSR				
All public libraries	962	1,340	963	6,139
Libraries of cultural organisations	256	931	616	5,060
These include:				
republican (ASSR), territorial & regional	2	58	2	256
district & neighbourhood	68	417	40	830
town	14	241	57	1,461
independent rural	160	164	478	2,033
independent children's	12	51	34	469
in club establishments	—	—	5	11

TABLE 14 (*continued*)

	1950		*1965*	
	Number of libraries	*Stock (in thousands)*	*Number of libraries*	*Stock (in thousands)*
Libraries of collective farms	592	191	184	372
Libraries of trade union organisations	92	114	134	597
Libraries of other departments and organisations	22	104	17	73
Armenian SSR				
All public libraries	1,467	2,239	1,166	8,628
Libraries of cultural organisations	1,301	1,896	1,053	7,977
These include:				
district & neighbourhood	39	125	33	743
town	38	361	101	2,580
independent rural	233	244	412	2,508
independent children's	60	212	55	986
in club establishments	931	954	452	1,160
Libraries of collective farms	43	35	9	19
Libraries of trade union organisations	77	152	95	610
Libraries of other departments and organisations	46	156	—	—
Turkmen SSR				
All public libraries	927	1,783	809	4,778
Libraries of cultural organisations	830	1,581	499	3,902

TABLE 14 (*continued*)

	1950		1965	
	Number of libraries	*Stock (in thousands)*	*Number of libraries*	*Stock (in thousands)*
These include:				
republican (ASSR), territorial & regional	1	24	1	57
district & neighbourhood	46	334	34	604
town	22	251	64	1,212
independent rural	153	238	347	1,285
independent children's	34	144	53	744
in club establishments	574	590	—	—
Libraries of collective farms	36	26	78	149
Libraries of trade union organisations	46	124	188	523
Libraries of other departments and organisations	15	52	15	133
Estonian SSR				
All public libraries	1,492	2,424	1,009	10,098
Libraries of cultural organisations	815	1,938	775	8,516
These include:				
district & neighbourhood	24	164	19	461
town	44	372	61	2,131
independent rural	734	1,354	654	5,200
independent children's	8	44	41	724
in club establishments	5	4	—	—

TABLE 14 (*continued*)

	1950		1965	
	Number of libraries	*Stock (in thousands)*	*Number of libraries*	*Stock (in thousands)*
Libraries of collective farms	366	101	16	54
Libraries of trade union organisations	285	356	154	1,355
Libraries of other departments and organisations	26	29	53	151

Let us give some data on the state of the book stocks of the public libraries of the cultural organisations. Here seventeen percent consist of social and political books, about four percent are books on natural sciences and scientific atheism, more than six percent are devoted to technology, six percent are concerned with agriculture and almost forty six percent to *belles lettres* or fiction. In public libraries of trade union organisations, the proportion of social and political books exceeds seventeen percent and *belles lettres* and fiction amounts to fifty percent.

During the years of Soviet administration, rich and varied stocks have been built up. Now, for every 100 people in the population, there are 454 books in public libraries, as against six in 1913, and ninety four in 1940. An even more significant change has occurred in rural areas, where in public libraries there are more than 450 books per 100 inhabitants, while in 1913 there were only three books, and in 1940 and 1950 there were forty nine and ninety one respectively. The provision of books for each person in the republics of Central Asia had particularly increased. The figures supplied in TABLE 16 reflect all these changes.

The rapid growth in economics, science, technology, literature and art, created a branching network of scientific, technical and other research libraries which helped in the solution of national economic problems. In the last ten years, the book stocks of these libraries have increased by more than 300 million copies, or almost 1·5 times. Moreover the stocks of libraries of scientific institutions, planning and construction organisations more than doubled, those of the libraries of medical institutions and sporting organisations have increased 1·9 times, those of the libraries of industrial, building and transport undertakings have increased 1·8 times, and those of libraries of professional, technical and higher educational institutions have increased 1·7 times. Incidentally, it should be mentioned that in conformity with the resolution of the Central Committee of the Communist Party ' On the state and measures for improving library affairs in the country ', the number of small libraries was somewhat reduced and the number of large ones (with book stocks of more than 10 thousand copies) was increased.

In technical and research libraries about four fifths of the stock consist of books and pamphlets and not more than a fifth of periodicals. In the majority of the scientific, technical, educational and reference libraries, foreign publications are well represented. In 1965, for example, of the 995 million copies of books and periodicals in technical and research libraries, 92 million consisted of foreign publications, or eleven percent of the total.

TABLE 15 : *Book stocks of public libraries of the Ministry of Culture according to the subject branches* (*at the beginning of 1966*)

| Books according to subject | Number of books and periodicals in all libraries | Libraries | | | | |
		Republic and regional	District and neigh-bour-hood	Town	Rural	Child-ren's
Social and political	127,009	13,083	18,338	27,297	58,899	9,392
Natural history and scientific atheism	27,761	4,606	3,384	6,163	9,525	4,083
Technical	47,372	19,714	4,065	9,314	10,291	3,988
Agricultural	46,626	3,145	6,208	2,642	33,120	1,511
Belles lettres and fiction	316,728	10,437	41,220	60,316	160,251	44,504
Art	26,314	3,309	3,278	6,318	9,636	3,773
For schools including classes I and II	95,503	253	4,119	6,833	47,046	37,252

TABLE 16: *The number of books and periodicals in public libraries on an average for every 100 of population*

	In towns and rural areas				In towns				In rural areas			
	1913	1940	1950	1965	1913	1940	1950	1965	1913	1940	1950	1965
USSR	6	94	134	454	17	186	199	453	3	49	91	455
RSFSR	7	112	155	476	23	209	219	454	4	59	103	508
Ukrainian SSR	5	88	115	503	13	172	178	507	4	44	80	497
Belorussian SSR	6	55	84	488	19	174	214	564	4	23	47	438
Uzbek SSR	—	37	51	205	—	92	96	273	—	19	31	168
Kazakh SSR	2	77	94	317	9	112	107	273	1	61	86	358
Georgian SSR	1	47	143	403	2	96	215	419	0·4	26	102	389
Azerbaijan SSR	1	78	143	396	2	161	202	398	0·4	29	95	395
Lithuanian SSR	1	20	102	569	6	63	106	526	0·3	7	100	604
Moldavian SSR	3	47	88	407	14	282	187	561	1	10	67	346
Latvian SSR	5	43	147	600	11	104	156	590	1	10	139	616
Kirghiz SSR	—	48	70	320	—	107	110	412	—	29	54	263
Tajik SSR	—	32	86	238	—	83	143	333	—	18	65	186
Armenian SSR	1	52	165	393	3	106	155	398	0·6	30	172	388
Turkmen SSR	—	93	146	250	—	129	173	348	—	73	128	155
Estonian SSR	3	93	220	786	20	98	173	565	2	90	266	1,155

A major change has taken place in the book stocks of technical and research libraries of the Union republics. As can be seen from TABLE 17, in comparison with 1957, the stocks increased 2·4 times in the Kirghiz SSR, almost double in the Azerbaijan and the Lithuanian SSRs, increased 1·8 times in the Kazakh SSR and increased 1·6 times in the Tajik and the Uzbek SSR. The growth in stocks in comparison with 1961 amounted to thirty percent over the country.

TABLE 17; *Growth in the stocks of technical and research libraries in the Union republics (at the beginning of the year)*

	Number of books and periodicals (million copies)		
	1957	1961	1965
RSFSR	444	498	641
Ukrainian SSR	108	116	153
Belorussian SSR	17	20	26
Uzbek SSR	15	18	23
Kazakh SSR	15	17	26
Georgian SSR	18	21	23
Azerbaijan SSR	8	12	15
Lithuanian SSR	10	11	19
Moldavian SSR	5	6	8
Latvian SSR	13	14	15
Kirghiz SSR	3	5	7
Tajik SSR	4	5	6
Armenian SSR	9	9	13
Turkmen SSR	5	6	7
Estonian SSR	9	10	13

The guaranteed supply of technical and specialist books to workers and employees is one of the indications characterising advances in the development of library affairs. The calculations show that in 1965, for every 100 workers and employees there were on an average 1,358 books and periodicals, as against 1,239 in 1961. In a number of Union republics these figures are higher: for every 100 workers and employees in 1965 in Estonia there were 2,389 books and periodicals, 2,260 in Lithuania, 2,246 in Armenia, 1,968 in Georgia, 1,780 in Turkmen, 1,754 in Latvia and 1,620 in Azerbaijan.

The development of economics and culture, the spread of the library network and the improvement of its work led to an increase in the number of readers. Even during the first years of Soviet rule, as our country was being reconstructed after the devastations of world and civil wars, the number of readers markedly increased. At the present time, Soviet libraries annually serve more than 100 million people.

Unfortunately we do not have available complete information of the number of readers in the libraries of pre-revolutionary Russia. Therefore we shall attempt to carry out some calculations beginning from the number of readers, on an average, using one public library in a specific province. Until the revolution, one public library served approximately 120-130 readers in a year. In 1911-1912, an average of eighty eight were served by the public (national) library of the Vologda province, 114 by the library of the Novgorod province, 138 by the Saratova province library and 133 by that of the Tver province. (It should be taken into account that these provinces lie in the central part of Russia.) Let us suppose that every public library in 1913 accommodated 130 readers, then the total of 13,876 public libraries in the pre-revolutionary period might have been about 2 million readers. In 1965, the public libraries of the country served 83 million readers.

From the early days of Soviet rule, all citizens, regardless of social status, had the right of free use of libraries. Already by 1925, public libraries alone served 5·5 million readers in the towns and country, and in 1930 they served almost 12 million (of them more than 7 millions used the town libraries and 4 millions used the rural libraries). In the following years, together with the growth in the number of libraries and an improvement in their activities, the number of readers considerably increased. Thus in 1940, 19 million readers were served by the independent libraries of organisations of national education (public libraries were then found in a department of the People's Commissariats for Education) who altogether in a year, were given more than 250 million books, pamphlets and periodicals. In 1960, independent public libraries of the Ministry of Culture were used by 53 million people, to whom more than 1 thousand million books were loaned, or on an average nineteen books per reader. In 1965, the readers of these libraries reached 63 millions.

133

Indicative of the activity of public libraries in the last three five year plans in the Union republics, we would like to mention that in the Ukraine, in 1965, 16 million readers were served which was four times greater than in 1960, and of the total number of readers more than 10 millions were served by the rural and district libraries. In Belorussia, in 1965, by comparison with 1950, the number of readers increased more than three times and the number of readers of independent rural libraries nine times. In Kazakhstan, in 1950, the number of readers amounted to 795 thousand and in 1965 they reached 2,681 thousand, which represents an increase of three hundred percent; the number of readers of independent rural libraries here increased eight times. The number of readers in other Union republics also considerably increased, especially in the Kirghiz, Tajik, Turkmen, Lithuanian and Azerbaijan SSRs (*see* TABLE 18).

TABLE 18: *Main indications of the work of public libraries of the Ministry of Culture in the union republics*

	1950			1965		
	All libraries	*including*		*All libraries*	*including*	
		district and neigh- bouring	*indepen- dent rural*		*district and neigh- bouring*	*indepen- dent rural*
RSFSR						
All readers (thousands)	15,063	4,645	3,793	34,578	5,182	14,199
Books and periodicals issued (thousands)	296,881	85,113	56,660	663,400	101,892	221,608
Average number of readers in one library	1,100	1,831	417	908	1,995	471
Average number of books read by one reader	20	18	15	19	20	16
Ukrainian SSR						
All readers (thousands)	3,929	1,097	987	15,599	1,398	9,174
Books and periodicals issued (thousands)	71,498	20,031	14,005	304,050	29,601	159,861
Average number of readers in one library	761	1,438	275	938	2,594	650
Average number of books read by one reader	18	18	14	19	21	17

134

TABLE 18 *(continued)*

| | 1950 | | | 1965 | | |
| | All libraries | *including* | | All libraries | *including* | |
		district and neigh-bouring	*indepen-dent rural*		*district and neigh-bouring*	*indepen-dent rural*
Belorussian SSR						
All readers (thousands)	636	235	113	2,053	261	933
Books and periodicals issued (thousands)	15,531	4,935	2,011	35,336	4,388	11,883
Average number of readers in one library	882	1,340	263	867	2,607	486
Average number of books read by one reader	24	21	18	17	17	13
Uzbek SSR						
All readers (thousands)	446	135	108	1,049	145	418
Books and periodicals issued (thousands)	5,019	1,076	479	15,925	2,220	4,054
Average number of readers in one library	743	1,019	310	635	1,039	354
Average number of books read by one reader	11	8	4	15	15	10
Kazakh SSR						
All readers (thousands)	795	290	169	2,681	281	1,396
Books and periodicals issued (thousands)	11,453	3,120	1,480	47,919	5,449	21,320
Average number of readers in one library	995	1,414	410	598	1,495	381
Average number of books read by one reader	14	11	9	18	19	15
Georgian SSR						
All readers (thousands)	438	69	75	1,050	141	444
Books and periodicals issued (thousands)	4,978	709	594	18,202	2,562	6,788
Average number of readers in one library	1,047	1,388	456	785	2,137	430

TABLE 18 *(continued)*

	1950			1965		
	All libraries	including		All libraries	including	
		district and neigh- bouring	indepen- dent rural		district and neigh- bouring	indepen- dent rural
Average number of books read by one reader	11	10	8	17	18	15
Azerbaijan SSR						
All readers (thousands)	431	62	78	1,017	104	438
Books and periodicals issued (thousands)	7,661	801	499	27,744	3,347	12,219
Average number of readers in one library	812	876	223	556	1,725	279
Average number of books read by one reader	18	13	6	27	32	28
Lithuanian SSR						
All readers (thousands)	273	64	140	1,103	89	783
Books and periodicals issued (thousands)	4,801	1,215	2,153	17,772	1,744	10,291
Average number of readers in one library	482	1,270	308	613	2,030	493
Average number of books read by one reader	18	19	15	16	20	13
Moldavian SSR						
All readers (thousands)	188	49	63	969	69	576
Books and periodicals issued (thousands)	3,439	875	633	14,006	1,201	6,134
Average number of readers in one library	450	815	210	961	2,877	658
Average number of books read by one reader	18	18	10	15	17	11
Latvian SSR						
All readers (thousands)	302	51	125	546	36	216
Books and periodicals issued (thousands)	7,488	1,243	2,039	14,963	1,293	3,642

TABLE 18 *(continued)*

	1950			1965		
	All libraries	*including*		*All libraries*	*including*	
		district and neigh- bouring	*indepen- dent rural*		*district and neigh- bouring*	*indepen- dent rural*
Average number of readers in one library	393	1,163	192	605	1,731	316
Average number of books read by one reader	25	24	16	27	36	17
Kirghiz SSR						
All readers (thousands)	215	80	52	777	70	413
Books and periodicals issued (thousands)	3,246	1,049	412	11,464	1,141	4,106
Average number of readers in one library	822	1,287	321	983	2,423	701
Average number of books read by one reader	15	13	8	15	16	10
Tajik SSR						
All readers (thousands)	83	29	29	266	32	135
Books and periodicals issued (thousands)	1,201	461	153	3,823	631	1,266
Average number of readers in one library	3,616	449	208	435	8,080	283
Average number of books read by one reader	14	16	5	14	19	9
Armenian SSR						
All readers (thousands)	219	33	76	467	43	167
Books and periodicals issued (thousands)	3,418	361	798	9,385	937	2,697
Average number of readers in one library	593	854	326	777	1,310	140
Average number of books read by one reader	16	11	11	20	22	16

137

TABLE 18 *(continued)*

	1950			1965		
	All libraries	*including*		*All libraries*	*including*	
		district and neigh- bouring	*indepen- dent rural*		*district and neigh- bouring*	*indepen- dent rural*
Turkmen SSR						
All readers (thousands)	82	24	22	221	22	85
Books and periodicals issued (thousands)	1,125	239	203	3,649	414	906
Average number of readers in one library	3,194	520	141	442	635	246
Average number of books read by one reader	14	10	9	16	19	10
Estonian SSR						
All readers (thousands)	212	27	122	438	32	172
Books and periodicals issued (thousands)	4,753	616	2,416	8,940	702	3,298
Average number of readers in one library	262	1,116	166	565	1,681	264
Average number of books read by one reader	22	23	20	20	22	19

In the last fifteen years, the stocks of libraries have continually increased. In 1950, on average, for each reader there were about six books, but in 1965 this figure again increased. In our country the main mass of readers was served by libraries having general book stocks. Thus in 1965, of 100 million readers, four fifths used public libraries, and approximately a fifth of the readers used technical and research libraries.

The Soviet people are active library users, annually reading ten library books each. Moreover many workers, collective farmers, employees, specialists and scholars have collections of books. In 1965, 2 thousand million printed works were issued to readers by the libraries of the country (apart from school libraries), and of these 1·5 thousand million copies were issued by public libraries. The extent of the activity of state public libraries in the last fifteen years has increased considerably (*see* TABLE 19).

More than 21 million readers were served by the public libraries of the trade union organisations in 1965; almost 390 million books being loaned.

Everywhere attention is drawn to the increase in the book issue in public libraries. On the whole, over the country in 1965, by comparison with 1950, book issues increased almost three times, and it increased more than four times in the Ukrainian SSR, 3·2 times in the Uzbek SSR, four times in the Kazakh and the Moldavian SSRs, 3·7 times in the Georgian SSR, 3·6 times in the Azerbaijan and the Kirghiz SSRs and almost four times in the Lithuanian SSR.

In 1950, rural libraries issued to readers in the whole of the USSR 85 million books; by 1965 the figure had risen to 470 million books, 5·6 times more. Let us recall that the rural population over this period decreased, their proportion being reduced from fifty percent at the beginning of 1961 to forty six percent at the beginning of 1966.

TABLE 19 : *Main indications of the work of independent public libraries of the Ministry of Culture*

	1950	1960	1965
In all the libraries			
All books and periodicals (millions)	137·7	581·0	761·5
All readers (millions)	23·3	53·0	62·8
Books and periodicals issued (millions)	442·5	1026·5	1196·6
Average number of books and periodicals in one library (thousands)	5·3	8·5	10·4
Average book provision per reader	5·9	11·0	12·1
Average number of readers in one library (thousands)	0·9	0·8	0·9
Average number of books read per reader	19·0	19·4	19·0
In regional, territorial & republic libraries			
All books and periodicals (millions)	23·6	47·6	67·0
All readers (millions)	1·6	1·7	2·1
Books and periodicals issued (millions)	36·4	41·9	48·4
Average number of books and periodicals in one library (thousands)	165·0	328·4	475·4
Average book provision per reader	15·0	27·8	32·6

TABLE 19 (*continued*)

	1950	1960	1965
Average number of readers in one library (thousands)	11·0	11·8	14·6
Average number of books read per reader	23·1	24·4	23·5

In district & neighbourhood libraries

	1950	1960	1965
All books and periodicals (millions)	38·1	82·5	90·3
All readers (millions)	6·9	8·0	7·9
Books and periodicals issued (millions)	121·9	157·3	157·5
Average number of books and periodicals in one library (thousands)	8·8	19·1	22·9
Average book provision per reader	5·5	10·3	11·4
Average number of readers in one library (thousands)	1·6	1·9	2·0
Average number of books read per reader	17·7	19·6	19·9

In town libraries

	1950	1960	1965
All books and periodicals (millions)	25·4	91·9	135·4
All readers (millions)	4·8	10·2	13·4
Books and periodicals issued (millions)	108·3	230·1	287·7
Average number of books and periodicals in one library (thousands)	13·5	23·7	26·8
Average book provision per reader	5·3	9·0	10·1
Average number of readers in one library (thousands)	2·5	2·6	2·7
Average number of books read per reader	22·7	22·6	21·5

In independent rural libraries

	1950	1960	1965
All books and periodicals (millions)	33·7	266·6	355·7
All readers (millions)	5·9	23·6	29·5
Books and periodicals issued (millions)	84·5	369·7	470·1
Average number of books and periodicals in one library (thousands)	2·0	4·8	6·0
Average book provision per reader	5·7	11·3	12·0
Average number of readers in one library (thousands)	0·3	0·4	0·5
Average number of books read per reader	14·2	15·7	15·9

TABLE 19 (*continued*)

	1950	1960	1965
In independent children's libraries			
All books and periodicals (millions)	16·9	92·4	113·1
All readers (millions)	4·1	9·5	9·9
Books and periodicals issued (millions)	91·4	227·5	232·9
Average number of books and periodicals in one library (thousands)	7·8	18·2	22·8
Average book provision per reader	4·1	9·7	11·4
Average number of readers in one library (thousands)	1·9	1·9	2·0
Average number of books read per reader	22·1	23·8	23·5

To present books to the reader the Soviet librarians organise branch libraries as well as issuing points and mobile libraries. Mobile libraries, which appeared active forms of service to readers in industrial undertakings, construction works and in communities, have become especially wide ranging. In 1965, of the total number of public libraries of cultural and trade union organisations, 70 thousand libraries had more than 300 thousand mobiles, *ie* an average four mobiles for each library. In the last fifteen years, the number of public libraries of cultural organisations having mobiles has increased by more than 43 thousand and the number of mobiles by 105 thousand. The network of mobile libraries has particularly grown in the country, and facilitates service to a considerably greater number of readers in the more remote areas. In 1950 the number of independent rural libraries, which had mobiles, amounted to little more than 8 thousand. By 1965 mobiles were attached to 47 thousand libraries, and in this time the number of mobiles increased from 32 thousand to 151 thousand or five times. Information regarding the work of mobile units in Union republics is given in TABLE 20.

In 1965, 72 thousand, or ninety percent, of the libraries in the system of the Ministry of Culture, organised 3·7 million activities of various kinds for popularising libraries: literary evenings, readers' conferences and bibliographic surveys (not counting exhibitions). On an average every library carried out in the year more than fifty activities of this kind. In addition state public libraries organised

1·7 million book and illustration exhibitions. This constitutes an increase of 300 thousand over 1960.

TABLE 20: *The number of independent public libraries of the Ministry of Culture having mobile libraries in 1965*

	Number of libraries	Those having mobile libraries attached	Number of attached mobile libraries
USSR	73,290	56,851	220,118
RSFSR	38,090	31,865	145,689
Ukrainian SSR	16,629	12,326	30,845
Belorussian SSR	2,366	1,936	7,694
Uzbek SSR	1,653	1,043	3,273
Kazakh SSR	4,481	3,353	9,288
Georgian SSR	1,339	760	2,184
Azerbaijan SSR	1,831	611	1,761
Lithuanian SSR	1,797	1,570	6,194
Moldavian SSR	1,008	848	2,934
Latvian SSR	902	839	3,541
Kirghiz SSR	708	605	3,377
Tajik SSR	611	147	568
Armenian SSR	601	278	1,135
Turkmen SSR	499	265	545
Estonian SSR	775	405	1,090

As the data in table 19 show, book issues grew continuously. However, all the book resources of our country are not yet fully used. This is shown, for example, by some reduction in turnover. The average turnover was reduced from 1·9 in 1955 to 1·6 in 1965 in the libraries of cultural organisations. The lowest turnover (less than 1) was observed in republic, territorial and regional libraries.

What is the cause of this position? It is submitted that in the first place it is the result of the rapid increase in book stocks. However it is undoubtedly a serious fault in the acquisitions policy of the library network. The book collections must be put in order and quickly weeded of obsolete and irrelevant literature. The coordination of acquisitions, and the work towards interlibrary agreements is not yet imposed everywhere. The scientific development of a standard for optimal stocks for different types of library is very important. Moreover librarians must apply the most effective forms of promotion to published material.

An important role in the service of books to the people and in the perfecting of the activities of the library is played by the librarian. In 1966, in the public libraries alone, 136 thousand qualified librarians, a number 2·3 times greater than in 1950, were employed.

TABLE 21 : *Number of qualified library workers in public libraries of all systems and departments* (*at the beginning of the year*)

	1951			1966		
	Total number	*including* in town libraries	in rural areas	Total number	*including* in town libraries	in rural areas
USSR	60,095	29,645	30,450	136,629	60,704	75,925
RSFSR	34,511	18,033	16,478	75,232	34,975	40,257
Ukrainian SSR	11,954	5,734	6,220	27,996	12,658	15,338
Belorussian SSR	1,865	1,042	823	4,531	2,171	2,360
Uzbek SSR	1,166	515	651	4,235	1,200	3,035
Kazakh SSR	1,673	763	910	7,513	2,266	5,247
Georgian SSR	1,774	795	979	2,459	1,093	1,366
Azerbaijan SSR	1,085	649	436	2,512	1,210	1,302
Lithuanian SSR	834	355	479	2,651	1,051	1,600
Moldavian SSR	672	229	443	1,949	656	1,293
Latvian SSR	1,027	363	664	1,753	920	833
Kirghiz SSR	491	210	281	1,587	533	1,054
Tajik SSR	392	102	290	1,011	311	700
Armenian SSR	1,213	363	850	1,227	700	527
Turkmen SSR	463	255	208	845	492	353
Estonian SSR	975	237	738	1,128	468	660

Besides this, there were about 60 thousand qualified librarians in technical and research libraries. According to the data of the all-Union school census (1961), more than 41 thousand trained librarians were employed in school libraries. Therefore there are 237 thousand trained librarians in all in the libraries of our country.

An active participation in library work is taken by volunteers. In 1966, in the independent public libraries of the Ministry of Culture system, the number of such volunteers amounted to more than a million, and in technical and research libraries more than 25 thousand people carried out library work voluntarily.

In TABLE 21 it is obvious that by 1965, by comparison with 1950, the number of library workers in public libraries had considerably increased. Thus in the whole USSR they increased 2·3 times, and by 2·5 times in rural areas; 4·5 times in the Kazakh SSR as a whole, and 5·8 times in the rural areas; 3·6 and 4·7 times in the Uzbek SSR as a whole and in its rural areas respectively; 3·2 and 3·8 in the Kirghiz SSR and in its rural areas, and 3·2 and 3·3 times respectively in the Lithuanian SSR and in its rural areas.

A considerable number of workers in libraries have higher and secondary education. In the 1965/66 school year, the number of students being trained in the library faculties of higher educational institutions consisted of about 23 thousand, and in technical schools more than 27 thousand persons were trained. Consequently in all in the past student year, almost 50 thousand people obtained higher and secondary library training. At the present time, the higher educational establishments and technical schools annually send out 10 thousand specialists in library science. In pre-revolutionary libraries paid librarians were almost non-existent. Teachers chiefly carried out library work in addition to their teaching duties. Thus in 1912, among the library workers on Vologda, Tver, Novogorod and Saratova and a number of other territories, teachers composed more than four fifths of the library workers, the proportion of paid librarians not exceeding twelve percent. Librarians in the provinces of tzarist Russia had an especially low educational level. In 1966, of 109 thousand librarians working in the public libraries of cultural organisations (not counting librarians of club libraries), more than 100 thousand, or ninety three percent, had higher or secondary education and of their number there were 15 thousand with higher education.

TABLE 22 clearly shows the increase in the educational level of librarians in all the Union republics. It is important to mention that during the years of Soviet rule the national staff of library workers increased in every republic. In the state libraries of the Georgian SSR, for example, higher and secondary education had been received by all library workers, in the Azerbaijan and Armenian SSRs, the number of librarians with higher and secondary education amounted to ninety eight percent, in Belorussia the proportion was ninety six per cent, in the Uzbek and Moldavian SSRs it was ninety five percent. In scientific, technical and other research libraries, the proportion of people with higher education is somewhat greater and amounts to approximately a third, and the total number of workers with higher and secondary education reaches ninety six percent.

TABLE 22: *Educational level of library workers in public libraries of the Ministry of Culture at the beginning of 1966 (in percentages)*

	Higher	Secondary
USSR	14	79
RSFSR	13	78
Ukrainian SSR	17	82
Belorussian SSR	16	80
Uzbek SSR	11	84
Kazakh SSR	8	77
Georgian SSR	32	68
Azerbaijan SSR	10	88
Lithuanian SSR	6	72
Moldavian SSR	13	82
Latvian SSR	12	78
Kirghiz SSR	13	84
Tajik SSR	4	85
Armenian SSR	18	80
Turkmen SSR	9	81
Estonian SSR	12	59

Figures in statistical surveys show the enormous advances in library affairs in our country during the years of Soviet administration. Tables, in which are grouped the indicators of library work during the main period of development of the Soviet state, give a picture of steady and very rapid growth, especially in the Union republics. The rapid and systematic development of the library network, the increase in the book stocks and the number of readers, all clearly confirm the cultural revolution as being accomplished in the USSR.

The five year plan (1966-1970) provides for the creation and development of a wide network of cultural institutions and a manifold improvement of cultural service to the population, especially in rural areas. There is outlined in particular an increase in the number of public libraries and clubs and the development of their material and technical foundation resources.

The analysis of the statistical data for the fifty years of Soviet administration helps us to plan the development of library affairs in our country during the period of the development of communism and to resolve the main trends, such as for example, the improvement in the use of the book stocks, the organisation of differentiated service to readers and perfection of the activities of scientific libraries and others.

LITERATURE REFERENCES AND NOTES

1 In the preparation of this paper the author has used material from the all-Union census of libraries 1934; statistical compilations *Narodnoe obrazovanie v SSSR po dannym tekushchikh obsledovanni na 1 yanvarya 1922, 1923, 1924 godov* (National education in the USSR according to data from inspections on 1 January, 1922, 1923 and 1924), Moscow, 1926; *Kul'turnoe stroitel'stvo SSSR* (Cultural development of the USSR), Moscow, 1940; *Kul'turnoe stroitel'stvo SSSR* (Cultural development of the USSR), Moscow, 1956; statistical annuals published by the Central Statistical Administration of the USSR *Narodnoe khozyaistvo SSSR* (National economy) for 1957-1965; statistical compilations *Dostizheniya Sovetskoi vlasti za 40 let v tsifrakh* (Achievements of Soviet rule after forty years, in figures), Moscow, 1957; *SSSR v tsifrakh* (USSR statistics) for 1960-1966, Moscow, 1961-1966; *Narodnoe khozyaistvo RSFSR v 1965* (National economy of the Russian Soviet Federated Socialist Republic in 1965), Moscow, 1966; *Narodnoe khozyaistvo Ukrainskoi SSR v 1965 godu* (National economy of the Ukrainian SSR in 1965), Kiev, 1966; *Narodnoe khozyaistvo Tadzhikskoi SSR v 1965 godu* (National economy of the Tajik SSR in 1965), Dyushambe, 1966; *Narodnoe khozyaistvo Litovskoi SSR v 1965 godu* (National economy of the Lithuanian SSR in 1965), Vilnius, 1966; *Narodnoe khozyaistvo Moldavskoi SSR v 1964 godu* (National economy of the Moldavian SSR in 1964), Kishinev, 1965; *Belorusskaya SSR v*

tsifrakh v 1965 godu (Belorussian SSR statistics in 1965), Minsk, 1966; *Sovetskaya Estoniya za 25 let* (Soviet Estonia during twenty five years), Tallin, 1965; *Kul'turnoe stroitel'stvo Azerbaidzhanskoi SSR* (Cultural development of the Azerbaijan SSR), Baku, 1961; *Kul'turnoe stroitel'stvo Armyanskoi SSR* (Cultural development of the Armenian SSR), Erivan, 1962; the periodical *Vestnik statistiki* 1961 (9), 1962 (1) and several other sources.

2 Detailed tables describing the library network on 1 October, 1934 are given in the paper: M M Poluboyarinov (Library affairs in the USSR. Statistics) in: *Bibliotechnoe delo v SSSR* (library affairs in the USSR), pages 76-79. Moscow, 1957.

3 For more details of the damage caused to library affairs during the war years, *see*: M M Poluboyarinov, *op cit*, pages 85-86.

4 For the detailed tables, reflecting the growth of the public library network and its stocks, *see*: M M Poluboyarinov, *op cit*, pages 91-93.

VII CATALOGUING PROBLEMS IN SOVIET LIBRARY SCIENCE

by Z N AMBARTSUMYAN

Up to the Revolution in Russia, much work was devoted to the production of catalogues. However, with few exceptions, technical questions took prime place of importance, and the compilation of the catalogue was considered separately from the basic question of library service to readers. Cataloguers widely discussed methods of constructing catalogues but in the description of published matter their contents were often ignored and the influence of catalogues on readers in the choice of books was disregarded.

A similar relation to the catalogue is clearly illustrated by the subjects considered at the first all-Russian Congress on Library Affairs convened in 1911. In the draft of ' The standard plan of establishing library techniques in small libraries ', worked out by the Commission of the Society of Library Science for national and community libraries, the problems of cataloguing were limited to the recording of the stock. In the section on ' Recording and storage of books ', it was shown that to facilitate ' the proper recording of the book stock, it is necessary to compile three types of entries ': a) a shelf-list; b) an alphabetic catalogue, and c) a systematic catalogue.[1]

In his paper, S D Maslovskii stated that in foreign and home library service, the view was widely taken that the catalogue entry was a simple record. The basis for this is the statement ' The reader is bound to know what book he needs. Most frequently it is a matter of merely looking in the catalogue to see whether we have such a book or not; and nothing more '.[2]

In the first years of the establishment of Soviet library science, this attitude to the catalogue did not change. The urgent tasks of developing the library network, the acquisition of stocks, the supervision of new readers and the search for active forms of promoting books, somewhat overshadowed the solution of cataloguing problems. In the party and government directives on the development of library affairs these problems were scarcely mentioned. Even problems of library classification were, to a large extent, concerned

148

with the arrangement of books on the shelves, rather than with the organisation of a classified catalogue.

In the program of work of the first all-Russian Library Congress in 1924, problems concerning organisation of library catalogues were not considered. However, at the all-Russian Bibliographic Congress, which took place in the same year, a discussion developed in connection with the creation of Soviet cataloguing rules. Strong arguments took place on the merits and disadvantages of the Decimal Classification and on the advisability of using determinants. The ideological side of catalogues appeared scarcely touched upon, only L N Tropovskii revealed the inadequacy of the Decimal system, especially in the field of the humanities, and the disparity of its construction with Marxist opinions.[3] The underestimation of the value of catalogues in making literature available led to marked deficiencies in the organisation of library service.

As far back as February 1919, Lenin, in a letter to Narkomproso, put forward ' The creation of central catalogues ',[4] as one of the most important areas of work, which libraries must have indicated in their reports. Even in August 1918, speaking at the first all-Russian Congress on national education, Krupskaia said: ' It is necessary to teach students the use of catalogues and indexes '. Little attention was paid to this side of library affairs, while instruction in the location of obscure books became a task of extreme importance.[5] In all her addresses to librarians Krupskaia described catalogues as an effective means of guidance in reading.

Nevertheless up to the end of the twenties many library workers still continued to differentiate between the instructional function of the librarian in work with readers, and the organisation of catalogues, which was regarded as a technical matter. This position was clearly expressed in the statement by I S Vugman commenting on the report by A I Kalishevskii on ' The classified and subject catalogue '. Vugman disapproved of attempts to connect the problem of catalogues with the common political aims of Soviet libraries: ' What is the topic of discussion? Catalogues of the scientific library. What is their purpose? Educational, pedagogical, agitational or philosophical? No. The purpose of them is to give scientific workers the books or groups of books they need.'[6]

However, by the time of the second all-Russian conference of scientific libraries (1926), in the address of the well known Soviet library expert, L V Trofimov, the need to begin compiling catalogues for readers[7] was voiced sufficiently clearly. The idea of readers being directed by means of a catalogue, and its important role in popularising books and guidance to reading, obtained final recognition after the decision of the Party Central Committee on the improvement of affairs of self education on 8 October 1933, and after the decision of the Central Investigation Committee on 27 March 1934, on ' Library affairs in USSR '. Entrusting to Soviet libraries important tasks in the development of self education and the advance of the cultural level of the workers, the party called on library workers to make wide use of book resources ' for the purpose of communism and for party political-educational work '.[8] Libraries would have to subordinate all branches of their activities to this task of political education and the advance of national culture.

At the conference on theoretical problems of library science and bibliography (December 1936), catalogues were described in close relationship with the educational and propaganda functions of libraries. Four papers were devoted to the problem of catalogues: B R Zel'tsle *Basic problems in the construction of the classified catalogue in a Soviet library;* G I Ivanov *The alphabetical catalogue in large scientific libraries;* A V Klenov *Systems and forms of catalogues in a public library;* and E I Shamurin *Centralised cataloguing in the USSR.*

In an address by B R Zel'tsle, the main requirements for library catalogues were expressed thus: ' The catalogues must be based on the Marxist-Leninist outlook, they must be imbued with Party principles. No "indifference to politics" or "abstract scientific character" may occur in catalogues.' The speaker was guided by Krupskaia's instruction to the effect that the Soviet librarian must disclose the stocks of a library from the point of view ' of the communistic valuation of books, of the selection of these books for a specific purpose, which we must give at the right moment to the staff '.[9]

A V Klenov also emphasised ' Unrelated to the type, whether it is a public or official catalogue, the content of entries, the formulation of headings, the method of classification of material and the titles of documents must be subordinated to the principle of the Bolshevik party '.[10]

After the conference of 1936, attention to catalogues as a means of popularising books and as a means of revealing the contents of the stock was intensified. Up to this time the alphabetic catalogue had been considered to be the basic and most important type, now the great role is discharged by catalogues in which the descriptions are grouped in relation to the contents of the books—under classified and subject headings. They now permitted libraries to be of real assistance in the self education of readers.

Even if it would be wrong to imply that failure arose from deep seated historical concepts, an advance in new ideas, establishing the close connection of catalogues with the educational tasks of the libraries, now took place smoothly. The previous formal relationship of catalogues has appeared repeatedly in recent years in the published works of various authors and in practice in libraries. In the classified catalogues of a number of libraries, the works of the founders of Marxist-Leninism received a limited representation (specifically in the case of works by Marx, Engels and Lenin). Additional index cards were not included in the sections corresponding to the themes of these works. The representation of Party documents was also limited and incomplete. Low qualifications and weak political training of a considerable number of staff compiling the catalogues made the latter sometimes not only useless, but confusing tools for readers.

The first edition of tables of the Decimal Classification, developed by L N Tropovskii (1938), gave much attention to the removal of ' rough deficiencies, flowing from the bourgeois outlook ' of the authors of the Decimal Classification. In all public libraries, the rearrangement of the classified catalogues in conformity with the new tables was begun. The Scientific Investigation Institute of Library Science and Bibliography was commissioned in 1939 to create a unified state code for the bibliographic description of printed publications. Subsequently this was made possible by the interlibrary cataloguing commission, which consisted of a number of highly qualified staff from Soviet libraries. Library workers realised the importance and necessity of relating catalogues to ideological aims.

Unfortunately, in the main, the important achievements in the realm of cataloguing, gained after thirty years, were not properly consolidated. Even in the post-war period, instructions were issued in which, as before, the ideological/political role of the catalogues was underestimated and their value in popularising books and guiding readers was underrated.

The governing body of the Moscow State Library Institute instructed the author of the present article to prepare a published report on library catalogues. According to the substance of the report read at the end of 1949, a brochure was published,[11] in which the great role of catalogues in the popularisation of the best works in print was pointed out, and the direct connection between the structure and contents of catalogues and the ideological tasks of the library was stressed. The presence in library stocks of obsolete publications required a purposeful approach to the selection of the books to be represented in the catalogues. A wider introduction of bibliographic methods into the compilation of catalogues was recommended, *ie* annotation of books with notes of critical value; of prime importance is the placing of entries for works by the founders of Marxist-Leninism and the decrees of the party and government, arranged alphabetically in the appropriate sections of a classified catalogue. It was mentioned that in the compilation of catalogues, especially in those of public libraries, it was advisable to use the recommended bibliographic indexes, standard catalogues, and bibliographical reviews of the best books and articles and lists of literature in academic courses. In compiling catalogues for readers, it is assumed that highly specialised and rapidly superseded books should be represented only in official catalogues. The relation between the contents of the literature and the construction of the catalogues, the type of library and its tasks in service to readers was established.

In textbook methods for the compilation of classified and subject catalogues, the necessity is all the more clearly shown for multi-aspect representation of the most scientifically important and valuable works in those branches and subject headings to which they have a direct relation. In alphabetical catalogues, additional descriptions and reference cards are used, ensuring a fuller disclosure of the stock.

In *Instructions concerning catalogues and cards for regional, provincial and republic (ASSR) libraries,* confirmed in 1959 by the Ministry of Culture, the role of library catalogues was clearly revealed and their value in all systems of library service to readers was definite; ' Catalogues in Soviet libraries are the basic means of revealing the stocks of libraries, providing information for readers as well as a means of active propaganda for the study of Marxist-Leninism, the decrees of the Communist party, Soviet government, and for political and scientific knowledge among a wide circle of library readers. The catalogues and cards of provincial, regional and republic (ASSR) libraries are the main reference and bibliographic tools by means of which a library actively assists the economic and cultural projects in provinces, territories and ASSRs (Autonomous Soviet Socialist Republics), informing party and Soviet organisations, undertakings, and scientific and cultural establishments of what is available in the library stocks and of newly received literature and providing them with bibliographic help.'[12] We find similar wording in *Instructions concerning catalogues for public libraries.*

We can see that the aims of library catalogues are closely connected with the basic aims of Soviet libraries. In books and articles published in recent years, views concerning the ideological value of library catalogues have been developed.[13] In connection with this it is important to remember the words of Krupskaia, who in 1926 spoke of the necessity to ' create conditions in which guidance to readers should not only be the responsibility of the librarian; it is important that the reader should be guided in the use of the catalogue and choose that book which he needs '.[14] Talking with the directors of the scientific and regional (provincial) libraries in 1937, Krupskaia said: ' The catalogue in scientific and public libraries is one of the most important things '.[45] At the present time library science sees in catalogues an active means of popularising books and guiding readers.

WORKING OUT PROBLEMS OF THE DESCRIPTION OF PUBLISHED MATERIAL

In the years preceding the Great October Revolution problems of bibliographic description were given only slight examination. In the few papers devoted to these problems, contradictory recommendations were given and international experience was insufficiently considered. The draft rules for national libraries may be considered the most important inclusions in 'The standard plan for the organisation of techniques in small libraries', discussed at the first all-Russian Conference on library affairs in 1911,[16] but these were still not put into practice. Public libraries did not have instructions giving specific methods for book description, but each of the great libraries compiled basic rules for themselves.

It is quite natural that even during the first year of Soviet rule, more attention was given to the question of book description. In the pages of the journal *Bibliotechnoe obozrenie* (Library review), versions of both the French and Italian instructions were published. Problems of book description were hotly discussed at the first all-Russian Bibliographic Conference, where, in spite of the contradictory opinions, the desire was expressed to create unified Soviet instructions, after a critical examination of foreign experience.[17]

For some years before the conferences in Petrograd and Moscow, special commissions carried out preparatory work on the compilation of instructions. As a result *Basic propositions for constructing a catalogue* was published in Petrograd in 1925,[18] in which the specific character of Soviet practice was considered to some extent. Thus the possibility of assuming the principle of the corporate author as a basis for description or cataloguing was disclaimed, although its use was recommended in the compilation of an auxiliary index to the catalogue. The Petrograd commission did not stick to one uniform descriptive entry, assuming it advisable in the catalogue to recommend entry under the first word of the title, and in the subject catalogue under the first noun. The commission began work in July 1922, at the Institute of Library Science, seeing as its task the creation of state instructions on book stocks. Into the Moscow commission, under the guidance of A I Kalishevskii, came G I Ivanov, E V Koreneva, L B Khavkina and later G K Derman, P Kh Kananov, L V Trofimov and E I Shamurin. Subsequently, because of the illness of A I Kalishevskii, the leadership of the commission resided with G I Ivanov. The Moscow commission gave preference to the Anglo-American instructions, but with amendments dictated by the practice of Soviet libraries. In a review of the book by E I

Shamurin, *Cataloguing,* A L Kalishevskii well expressed this position by stating ' It is without doubt that the basis of these rules (Anglo-American instructions) finds successful application in Russian cataloguing, but also we do not doubt that Russian practice shows the necessity to introduce some changes into these rules, necessitated by the basic conditions of our way of life '.[19]

The full work of the Moscow commission was published in 1928.[20] It should be mentioned that the principle of the corporate author was applied in practice by 1923 but was finally legalised later.[21] Discussion of many problems of book description in catalogues and bibliography continued in the pages of the Soviet periodical press at the end of the twenties and the beginning of the thirties. Problems of the principle of entry under corporate authors, of the fullness of the entry, of the use of standard descriptions for various types and forms of catalogues, and of the language of the description[22] give rise to animated discussion.

At a conference in 1936 on the theoretical problems of library science and bibliography, the decision was taken to begin compiling the practical handbook necessary to secure compulsorily uniform entries in catalogues, in all types of library. In 1939 this work was entrusted to the Scientific Investigation Institute of Library Science and Reference Bibliography. In 1941, in connection with the liquidation of the Institute, a cataloguing commission was organised in Moscow by the State Library Institute from representatives of the largest libraries in the country and the All-Union Book Chamber. In 1942, the People's Commissariat of Education of the RSFSR ordered a new structure for the inter-library cataloguing commission, which was required to prepare official state instructions on book cataloguing. Representatives of the largest research libraries in the country, the Moscow Library Institute and the All-Union Book Chamber were incorporated into the Commission, and from this period the Commission worked with the V I Lenin State Library of the USSR. In 1949 the first volume of instructions *Common rules on the inventory of printed documents for library catalogues* (no 1, part 1, *Inventory of books*), was published. Among several authors are N Ya Gorbachevskaya, I N Emel'yanova, E A Novikova, L V Trofimov, E I Shamurin and other obvious specialists in the field of cataloguing. In the following ten years (1949-1958), issues of *Com-*

mon rules, including rules of cataloguing for other forms of printed documents, were published.[23]

As already mentioned, Soviet library scientists strove to create a common instruction for the description (inventory) of printed works for catalogues of all types of libraries. However, in the process of the development of *Common rules,* it became clear that complete uniformity of the rules of cataloguing for research and public libraries was not possible. The reason for this is correctly explained by E A Novikova, one of the authors of *Common rules,* who said ' With the differences in composition and size of their stocks and also of the inquiries, in which the different approaches of library readers were reflected in the use of the catalogues, it was necessary to elaborate the various instructions, although these were based on the common principles '.[24]

After publication of the first part of the above named edition, the commission set about preparing instructions for the cataloguing of books in public libraries, the draft of which was finished and printed in 1950.[25] It was widely discussed in library circles, and many remarks and suggestions from technicians and research workers were received. In 1953, the first and in 1954, the second, edition of rules for public libraries[26] were published. In 1955 instructive/systematic directions *On the organization of alphabetical catalogues in rural, regional and town libraries* was published, and in 1964 *Rules for the description of books and the composition of an alphabetical catalogue for rural libraries* appeared.

Thus, Soviet scientific and public libraries obtained official instructions for the description of published literature for library catalogues. These were the results of the fruitful efforts of a large collection of specialists and practising librarians.

The development of rules of entries for various types of bibliographic publications was a no less important task. Moreover the specific character of the list should be considered, and that which is appropriate should conform as far as possible with the rules for entries in library catalogues, since in bibliographic practice, library catalogues are used as sources of information on the literature, but cataloguers are often obliged to define more accurately the information about publications to be listed in bibliographic sources.

In 1964 *Rules for bibliographic description of printed publications* was published by the Library of the Academy of Sciences, USSR.[27] Comparing this publication with *Common rules for the inventory of printed documents for library catalogues,* it becomes clear that a considerable advance was made by the use of common elements in the rules for catalogues and bibliographic entry.

The publication of the items named above did not denote the end of the work in perfecting effective rules. Constant investigation of existing practices in the composition and use of the catalogue by libraries and readers made it possible to show the deficiencies and inaccuracies in the content and formulation of the rules for entry. On this basis, the inter-library cataloguing commission regularly reviewed the rules. In 1959 the publication of a bi-annually corrected and supplementary edition of *Common rules*[28] began. New editions of *Common rules for small libraries,* and also a second edition of the second part of *Common rules* titled *Description of periodical publications* were printed.[29]

The great events of recent years in the development of the theory of cataloguing were shown by the scientific conference on cataloguing convened in 1965 in Moscow. Representatives of 171 libraries of the USSR took part in its work. In the plenary and sectional meetings of the conference, papers by V A Vasilevskaya—*The stages and perspectives in the development of cataloguing,* and by E A Novikova—*Common principles and the specific character of cataloguing of printed material for various types of libraries of the USSR,* and scientific reports on the multiple problems of the description of various forms of published material in library catalogues and bibliographies were listened to and discussed. The whole conference indicated the high theoretical level of development of the principles of book description in our country.[30]

SOLVING PROBLEMS OF THE THEORY AND PRACTICE IN LIBRARY CLASSIFICATION

Before the October Revolution, the majority of library scientists and practical workers pointed out the weak points in the state of classified catalogues in libraries in Russia. In urban and rural public libraries it was common to find in use a short, arbitrarily compiled, scheme of classification in which not even major branches of science were separated, which consequently hampered the classified display of the stocks.

157

The position was no better in research libraries. Even in the Rumyantsevskii Museum there was no classified catalogue except of foreign literature; a million books in the stock of the Russian section were revealed only in an alphabetic catalogue. The main cause hampering the production of classified catalogues in research libraries was the general absence of an acceptable library classification scheme.

At the beginning of the twentieth century, a large number of offshoots of the Decimal Classification appeared (especially its second Brussels' variant) and were suggested for use in our own libraries. This suggestion was discussed at the 1911 conference, but was declined although the Decimal Classification was described as 'meriting attention'. Nevertheless, owing to the necessity for the compilation of classified catalogues, the Decimal Classification began to be applied in many urban and some large research libraries during the first decade of the twentieth century.

The revolutionary reconstruction of the whole system of library service dating from the first days of Soviet rule demanded the display of library stocks according to their content. The alphabetical catalogue might, to some degree, satisfy the inquiries of a comparatively narrow circle of readers who turn to the library for books they knew. For a widely read public broadening their knowledge, catalogues were necessary in which books were grouped according to their subject matter. However, the construction of a well organised classified catalogue, easily accessible to all, was obviously impossible without an accepted classification scheme.

The Decimal Classification attracted library workers by the simplicity and convenience available in its indexes. Moreover it was already in part practically tested in a number of pre-revolution libraries. Although its ideological faults were also mentioned in print, they became relegated to second place.[31] In many towns, abridged and partially extended tables of Decimal Classification were issued for public libraries. Since these editions were often badly coordinated and many indexes had different meanings, confusion arose in the organisation of classified catalogues and in the arrangement of books on the shelves. In 1921, the Chief Political Education Authority's decision was published on 'the necessary transfer of all libraries of the RSFSR to the Brussels international system of the Decimal Classification'. In this same year the first official publication of tables of the Decimal Classification came into existence.[32]

Thus the Decimal system was authorised in Soviet libraries. It was used in the first place because the creation of a new Soviet classification in a short period of time was impossible and there was very great necessity for the unification of stocks and catalogues. Use of the Decimal Classification at that stage was of great value. Uniformity in the classification of books in all public libraries, greater efficiency in the use of library staffs, centralised cataloguing and the use of the Universal Decimal Classification on printed cards (1952), was all made possible thanks to the use of a single classification scheme by libraries.

However, in the decision of the Chief Political Education Authority, the compulsory use of the Decimal Classification for all libraries was mentioned, while published tables were insufficiently detailed for the classification of the huge stocks of the great libraries. Changes introduced into the tables were often of a very general character. Many very important problems of Soviet life, which were reflected in the literature, were sometimes not revealed by the indexes to this classification whose foundations were so faulty. In practice, this system was not employed in research libraries. There were, however, a small number of exceptions.

Even at the first all-Russian Bibliographic Congress, a discussion developed on the advisability of the compulsory use of the Decimal Classification. Not all specialists confessed to the ideological unsoundness of the Decimal Classification. Thus N N Orlov stated that it was a system which was practical and not philosophical ' and therefore any attempt to consider ' the Decimal Classification from what is, or was, the ideological point of view, was fundamentally wrong. He said that in a library scheme it was only important for printed material on one subject to be grouped in one place, ' all equal and necessarily the same '.[33] L N Tropovskii at this stage clearly defined the relation of Soviet science to the Decimal Classification: ' Nobody objects to a Decimal system as a method. We object to the present system of this classification.'[34] Many of the speakers supported this idea. The Congress turned to the Chief Political Education Authority with a request not to consider the use of the Decimal Classification obligatory. In the resolution, the necessity for revision of the system was also mentioned.[35]

The shortcomings of the classification for the tasks of Soviet libraries, and with the content of literature in their stocks, gave rise to the possibility of changing the classified catalogue for a dictionary one. For example, D A Balika, in her paper on the dictionary catalogue, began with the statement ' It is no secret that the dictionary catalogue is the most democratic of all methods of bringing books to the notice of readers '.[36] At the end of the twenties, in the periodical *Krasnyi bibliotekar,* an account was given of ' The introduction of the dictionary catalogue into libraries ', in which a report was made about the setting up of a conference on rationalisation of library work, by A A Pokrovskii, with subsequent discussion upon it. The main points of the report were expounded further in ' The introduction of the dictionary catalogue into the libraries of the Political Education Administration and the trade unions is an urgent matter,' ' In the reorganisation of libraries, the dictionary catalogue is preferable '.[37]

It is characteristic that at the second all-Russian Conference of science libraries, three papers were presented on the dictionary catalogue and not one on classification or the classified catalogue. Among a large part of library staffs the opinion prevailed that the classified catalogue was outdated and in changing it, the dictionary catalogue must be used.

At the end of the twenties, in order to restore the authority of the Decimal system and satisfy the requirements of large (mainly research) libraries in the classification of their stocks, fuller tables of this scheme were published, making detailed corrections and additions to its structure. However these particular readjustments were not able to eliminate the main defects, namely the deep-seated disparity of this classification system with the new phenomena of the community life of our country. A radical review of the Decimal Classification was only completed in 1938 with the publication of Decimal Classification tables revised by L N Tropovskii.[38] Here sections of social/political literature, philosophy and history were again revised and the formulation of headings was reviewed in conformity with Soviet practice.

With the incorporation of this scheme into practice, the discussion of cataloguing problems was assisted at the conference on theoretical problems of library science and bibliography in 1936. In his paper, B R Zel'tsle spoke on the great value of a classified catalogue, which was the fundamental and true catalogue of a Soviet library.

Recommended for use by the Library Administration of the People's Commissariat of Education these tables laid the foundations for reconstruction of the classified catalogues of public libraries and, with some additions and changes introduced in the postwar years, are widely used up to the present day in town and district libraries, and from 1963 in regional and in some research libraries.[39]

The tables revised by L N Tropovskii solved to a large extent the problems of creating a classified catalogue in Soviet public libraries. However in this edition, it was impossible to remove completely the errors of the Decimal Classification. The artificiality and random character found in the order of the main classes and their important sub-divisions unavoidably introduced discrepancies with the ideological-educational aims of the Soviet libraries. An urgent need arose for the development of a Marxist-Leninist library/bibliographic classification scheme and in the construction of a classified catalogue in conformity with it.

Such work was begun in the thirties by the V I Lenin State Library of the USSR. Much more followed in the post-war years. The M E Saltykov-Shchedrin State Public Library, the Library of the Academy of Sciences, USSR, and the All-Union Book Chamber also helped in this work. In 1959, the Ministry of Culture of the RSFSR formed a commission from representatives of science libraries. A number of the main classes of the new classification and the secondary divisions of these classes were approved. For the first time in history, a library classification was constructed on the basis of the Marxist-Leninist classification of science and in conformity with the ideals of advanced Soviet science.

In 1960, the publication of a new library/bibliographic classification began in separate parts. At the end of 1966, twenty five parts were published embracing all the branches of the natural sciences, technology and also some branches of social science. The work is not finished. The scientific validity of the tables was guaranteed by

161

the work of the most outstanding Soviet scientists in the development of the classification system. The new scheme received approval in scientific establishments and was partly used in some science libraries.[40] The only doubts expressed were in the correctness of the method of indexing chosen by the compilers. Opponents pointed out that the use of the letters of the Russian alphabet and the unnecessary complexity of the indexes to the sections posed practical problems in the use of the system (especially in those national regions of our country which employ other scripts).[41] At present the possibilities are being studied of consolidating the indexes and changing the letters to numbers, preserving the logical construction already achieved and the scientific validity of the divisions. At the end of 1965 the Board of the Ministry of Culture examined the new classification and decided on the advisability of using it as a common system. The set task for the next few years is the compilation of alternative editions for libraries of different types, including public libraries.

After the incorporation of the new system into library practice, the All-Union Book Chamber contemplated carrying out centralised classification in conformity with it, with the help of printed cards. The Ministry of Culture of the RSFSR gave instructions to acquaint all library school students with the new classification, with the possibilities of its application and use in the compilation of bibliographic handbooks. Similar instructions were received by library schools as well as cultural and educational institutes having library sections.

Therefore the commemoration of the fiftieth anniversary of the Great October Revolution sees completed work of great importance in the development of library affairs and bibliography in our country, as well as the establishment of a classification system satisfying the modern level of scientific knowledge. We understand that the incorporation of the new Universal Classification into the practice of libraries of all departments and types demands great effort and expense, but the scheme already has a firm foundation.

THE THEORY OF ARRANGING PRINTED MATERIAL BY SUBJECT AND THE DICTIONARY CATALOGUE

In the cataloguing practice of Soviet libraries, the dictionary catalogue is a supplementary aid being used particularly in science libraries. In the Report of B R Zel'tsle mentioned earlier, at a conference on the theoretical problems of library science and bibliography (1936), the value of the dictionary catalogue was defined as selective (not including all the library stock). This position was the basis of instructions on catalogues and card indexes for libraries of various types. A relatively large number of libraries in our country use the dictionary catalogue for all their stock. For example, medical libraries, for which the medical classification scheme used by us has shown little and unsuccessful development. Nevertheless libraries formed in the twenties when, as already mentioned earlier, the dictionary catalogue had gained importance, having once created a dictionary catalogue, continued to use it up to the present time as the only full catalogue.

Other libraries (for example, the State Public Historical Library of the Russian Soviet Federated Socialist Republic), first created a dictionary catalogue of all the stock and later changed it to a classified catalogue.

It must be pointed out that in the majority of cases at the present time, dictionary catalogues are compiled and used in special libraries for only part of the stock, in accordance with their needs, together with a classified catalogue of all the stock.

The spread of the dictionary catalogue is relatively less and the attention to problems of the theory of dictionary cataloguing and the dictionary catalogue is correspondingly less. In a bibliography, Yu I Masanova has counted only ninety four titles of books and papers on the dictionary catalogue and dictionary cataloguing, of which seventy two appeared in the prewar period.[42] About ten works (mainly published in the twenties and thirties) were devoted to a comparison of the classified and dictionary cataloguing systems. If it is reckoned that the total number of works reflecting problems of catalogues totals 1,430, then in reality literature on the dictionary catalogue for forty years is very sparse.

It must, however, be mentioned that in recent years interest in dictionary cataloguing has somewhat revived. Periodicals have contained a few papers in which the authors show unfounded disregard for the classified catalogue. During the three years (1963-1965), in the collected papers *Sovetskaya bibliografiya* (Soviet bibliography), about ten papers were published in which some authors proposed a wider application of dictionary catalogues. In the collected papers *Tekhnicheskie biblioteki SSSR* (Technical libraries of the USSR) a discussion on subject treatment and the organisation of dictionary catalogues was reported. In the post-war years dissertations on the dictionary catalogue (M N Konovalova, E V Marchenko and K I Rudel'son) were defended and papers by Ya M Dikovskaya, S G Karpova and L G Volgar were published containing valuable theoretical suggestions on subject treatment and systematic instructions for the dictionary catalogue. On the basis of many years of practice in maintaining a dictionary catalogue, lists of subject headings for medical literature (State Central Scientific Medical Library—1958) and technical literature were compiled and published. The theory and practice of subject treatment were developed in the Fundamental Library of Social Sciences of the Academy of Sciences USSR, which published lists of dictionary headings based on the literary warrant of socialist/political literature as well as collected papers on problems of the dictionary catalogue.

In recent years the Soviet theory of subject treatment, resting on experiments in maintaining dictionary catalogues in large Soviet libraries, has received considerable advancement. The logical bond existing between the theory and technique of subject treatment and the development of information search systems of a descriptive type is very promising in this respect. Great consideration is given in the Soviet and foreign press to information retrieval systems and many authors also recognise the necessity of using subject analysis in development of information retrieval systems. In collected papers issued by the State Committee for Chemical Industry,[43] among a number of sources for compiling dictionaries of descriptive terms together with specially compiled glossaries, mention is made of ' large subject indexes and catalogues of scientific/technical libraries ' (for example, indexes to *Chemical abstracts* and *Chemisches Zentralblatt*). Section IV of this collection is completely devoted to the use of the principles of subject indexing for the creation of thesauri of descriptive terms.[44]

The development of a retrieval system from descriptive terms is based on the theory and method of descriptive terminology and the dictionary catalogue. However the dictionary catalogue and descriptive terminology, in whatever form they have evolved up to recent

164

years, have not lost their significance. The traditional form of card catalogues now serves as the most important source of information. Practice in their use will doubtless stimulate further development of the theoretical basis of subject cataloguing and indexing.

RESULTS OF THE THEORY AND PRACTICE OF CATALOGUING DURING THE LAST FIFTY YEARS

During the fifty years of Soviet library development, the solution to the theoretical problems of cataloguing was closely connected with the urgent requirements of library practice. Many years of practice in the maintenance of library catalogues of different forms and types in Soviet libraries, many possessing enormous and differing stocks, have helped a large number of librarians to solve these problems. The close connection between the Soviet theory of catalogues and the continuously improving practices in their maintenance in libraries must be mentioned. At the same time, the theoretical position in the field of cataloguing was constantly checked by practice, and the most effective methods were introduced and satisfactorily operated in libraries. Due to this, appreciable results were obtained in the organisation and use of library catalogues, which actively entered into the system of service to readers.

Libraries of all types and forms are now provided with a system of help in bibliographic control. *Common rules* of description for printed works for large scientific and public libraries, which have been mutually agreed upon led to conformity of entry in the catalogue. Entries in catalogues agree with the entries of books in bibliographical sources.

The scientific conference on cataloguing, which took place in the V I Lenin State Library in 1965, made considerable contributions to the theory of book description, outlining ways of solving many difficult problems facing libraries.

The Soviet theory of cataloguing merited appreciation from abroad. At the International Conference on Cataloguing Principles which took place in Paris in October 1961, the basic position formulated in the report of the inter-library cataloguing commission received approval[45] and exerted a certain influence on the practice of book description in other countries.

Marked advances were also achieved in the field of classification

165

of printed material. Unity of the tables of the Universal Decimal Classification, prepared in accordance with Soviet practice, which are used in regional, public and children's libraries has been ensured. The completion of the development of the new Soviet library/bibliographical classification by the collective efforts of the large science libraries under the direction of the Ministry of Culture of the Russian Federation is of great value. In accordance with the decision of the Board of the Ministry of Culture, measures are now being taken to introduce the new classification into the practices of different types of libraries by means of parallel editions.

As already mentioned, in recent years marked progress has been made in the development of the theoretical basis of the dictionary catalogue and subject terminology for printed works. Discussions on the dictionary catalogue and its place in the system of catalogues in Soviet libraries, will doubtless show a beneficial influence on the practice of maintaining dictionary catalogues and on developing methods of subject analysis.

Problems of coordinated systems of catalogues in libraries of different types were first raised at a conference on theoretical problems of library science and bibliography (1936). Studies by Soviet library scientists made it possible to produce scientifically valid instructions ensuring uniformity in the construction and interrelationship of efficient catalogues.

In papers of recent years and in instruction manuals, compulsory methods for Soviet libraries are outlined for the direct disclosure in catalogues of the most important printed works by systematic and scientific methods.

Scientifically based solutions to the most important problems of book description, classification and subject treatment as well as the regularisation of catalogue compilation made possible the solution of problems found in centralised cataloguing and classification. For more than forty years issues of printed cards, classified according to the tables in use and using subject heading, were produced by the All-Union Book Chamber and the V I Lenin State Library. Printed cards for public libraries were distributed on subscription in four complete sets, intended for town, regional, country and children's libraries. It is possible for research libraries to receive both a full set for the whole of book production issued by a publisher, and also to receive the sectional sets appropriate to the needs of the special library. Centralised cataloguing and classification at source has been implemented. The majority of the publishers now print the classification symbol on the back of the title page. Inter-republic technical publishing agreements have great significance in the publishing world.[46] In accordance with this document, from 1 April 1967, all publishers in the country are required to indicate on the back of the title page the classification number of all books destined for public libraries, or on the back cover of the book to print a copy of the annotated catalogue card entry, including the full library entry together with the description and annotation.[47] It is difficult to overestimate the value of these recommendations for libraries. The information in a book, most important for the organisation of libraries, permits its entry in all the available catalogues on the day of its acquisition with the least expenditure of energy or time. The next organisational task is to supply the acquisitions department of the library with tools permitting the reproduction, on index cards, of the bibliographic entries shown in the books and to guarantee libraries the necessary number of copies.

By tracing the path of development of the Soviet theory of catalogues and the compilation and use of catalogues in libraries, conclusions can be drawn concerning the effective links between theory and the actual work of Soviet libraries. Library catalogues, compiled on an authentic scientific basis, successfully fulfil the task of prompt information and active popularisation of the best publications. Henceforth, efforts will have to be concentrated on the many unsolved tasks of library catalogues. By the decision of the Council of Ministers, on 29 November 1966, the Ministry of Culture assumed responsibility for further perfecting scientific information work in all general libraries, so that the widest use may be made of their extensive stocks. The solution of this important problem requires the introduction of mechanisation into the compilation and use of catalogues, more intensive development of a system of combined catalogues, and the conducting of investigations to study the effective use of catalogues by readers. The problem of our use of catalogues has so far received little investigation. Only in recent years has work been carried out under the direction of the Commission formed by the Ministry of Culture of the RSFSR on the

167

problems of the library and scientific information. The interest in this work shown by the largest libraries in the country makes it possible to expect valuable results for Soviet libraries, which will assist subsequent development in the theory and practice of maintaining catalogues.

LITERATURE REFERENCES AND NOTES

1 *Trudy pervogo Vserossiiskogo s'ezda po bibliotechnomu delu* (Proceedings of the first all-Russian Congress on library affairs) page 261. St Petersburg, 1912.

2 *Ibid,* page 120.

3 *Trudy pervogo Vserossiiskogo bibliograficheskogo s'ezda* (Proceedings of the first all-Russian bibliographic conference) page 66. Moscow, 1926.

4 *Lenin o bibliotechnom dele* (Lenin on library affairs), page 62. Moscow, 1960 [Translated in S Simsova *ed*: *Lenin, Krupskaia and libraries,* pages 20-21. Bingley, 1968.]

5 N K Krupskaia: *O bibliotechnom dele, Sbornik* (Library affairs. Collected papers), page 112. Moscow, 1957.

6 *Trudy pervoi konferentsii nauchnykh bibliotek RSFSR* (Proceedings of the first conference of scientific libraries of the Russian Soviet Federated Socialist Republic), page 187. Moscow, 1926.

7 *Trudy vtoroi vserossiiskoi konferentsii nauchnykh bibliotek* (Proceedings of the second all-Russian conference of scientific libraries), pages 187, 215-216. Leningrad, 1929.

8 *Zolotoi fond sovetskoi kul'tury* (Golden stock of Soviet culture) *Pravda.* 12 April 1935.

9 *Vopros o katalogakh. Materialy dlya obsuzhdeniya na soveshchanie teoreticheskim voprosam bibliotekovedeniya i bibliografii, 16-27 Dekabrya 1936* (The problem of catalogues. Subjects for consideration at the conference on the theoretical problems of library science and bibliography, 16-27 December 1936), page 3. Moscow, Vsesoyuz kniga palata, 1936.

10 *Vopros o katalogakh* (The problem of catalogues), page 23.

11 Z N Ambartsumyan: *Rol i znachenie katalov sovetskikh bibliotek* (Role of the catalogues of Soviet libraries). Moscow, Goskul'tprosvetizdat, 1951.

12 *Sbornik rukovodyashchikh materialov po bibliotechnoi rabote* (Collected papers on guidance materials in library work), page 188. Moscow, Vsesoyuz kniga palata, 1963.

13 To name a few of their papers; D K Zhak and S M Smirnova: *Katalogi raionnoi i gorodskoi biblioteki* (Catalogues of regional and town libraries). Moscow, Gos biblioteka SSSR imeni V I Lenina, 1957; Z N Ambartsumyan: (N K Krupskaia and library catalogues) *Uchenye zapiski (Mosk gos bibliotech inst)*, 1959 5 pages 61-72; B Yu Eidel'man: (N K Krupskaia on library catalogues) *Trudy (Leningr gos bibliotech inst)*, 1959 6 pages 97-102.

14 N K Krupskaia: *O bibliotechnom dele. Sbornik* (Library affairs. Collected papers), page 479. Moscow, 1957.

15 *Ibid,* page 363.

16 *Trudy pergovo Vserossiiskogo s'ezda po bibliotechnomu delu* (Proceedings of the first all-Russian congress on library affairs), part 2, pages 260-310. St Petersburg, 1912.

17 *Trudy pervogo Vserossiiskogo bibliograficheskogo s'ezda* (Proceedings of the first all-Russian bibliographic congress) pages 93-103. Moscow, 1926.

18 *Bibliotechnoe obozrenie,* pages 58-73. 1925 2.

19 *Krasnyi bibliotekar,* page 95. 1925 7.

20 *Instruksiya po sostavleniyu alfavitnogo kataloga. I -Materialy Instituta bibliotekovedeniya* (Instructions for compiling an alphabetic catalogue. Part 1, —work of the Institute of Library Science), pages 1-56. Moscow, Gos biblioteka SSSR imeni V I Lenina, 1928.

21 G K Derman and others: *Instruktsiya po katalogizatsii proizvedenii kollektivov* (Instructions for cataloguing publications of corporate authors. Moscow, Gos tsentr kniga palata RSFSR, 1926.

22 N Ya Torbachevskaya and E A Novikova: in *Bibliotechnoe delo v SSSR* (Library affairs in USSR), pages 261-293. Moscow, 1957.

23 *Edinye pravila opisaniya proizvedenii pechat dlya bibliotechnykh katalogov* (Common rules for the description of published material for library catalogues).

No 1, part 1. Description of books. Moscow, 1949.

No 1, part 2. Organisation of an alphabetic catalogue of books. Moscow, 1952.

No 2. Description of periodical publications. Leningrad, 1954.

No 3. Description of cartographic publications. Leningrad, 1950.

No 4. Description of music publications. Moscow, 1952.

No 5. Description of printed drawings. Moscow, 1958.

No 6. Special forms of technical publications. Moscow, 1957.

24 E A Novikova: (Unity of principles and the specific character of the cataloguing of printed publications for the different types of libraries in the USSR) *Sodoklad na nauchnoi konferentsii po katalogizatsii* (Reports on the scientific conference on cataloguing), page 3. Moscow, 1965.

25 *Edinye pravila po opisaniya proizvedenie pechati dlya katalogov massovykh bibliotek i bibliograficheskikh ukazetelei. Proekt dlya obsuzhdeniya* (Common rules for the description of published material for catalogues of public libraries and bibliographic indexes. Project for discussion). Moscow, 1950.

26 *Edinye pravila po opisaniya proizvedenie pechati dlya katalogov nebol'shikh bibliotek i bibliograficheskikh ukazatelei* (Common rules of description of published material for catalogues of small libraries and bibliographic indexes). Moscow, 1953; second edition, Moscow, 1954.

27 N A Nikiforovskaya: (compiler) *Pravila bibliograficheskogo opisaniya proizvedenii pechati. Posobie dlya bibliografov, nauchnykh i izdatel'skikh rabotnikov* (Rules of bibliographic description of published material. Textbook for bibliographers, scientific workers and publishers), edited by S P Luppova. Leningrad, Biblioteka Akad Nauk SSSR, 1964.

28 *Edinye pravila opisaniya proizvedenii pechati dlya bibliotechnykh katalogov, ch 1 Opisanie knig* (Common rules for the description of printed material for library catalogues, part 1. Description of books), second edition. Moscow, Gos biblioteka SSSR imeni V I Lenina, 1959.

29 *Edinye pravila opisaniya proizvedenii pechati i organizatsii alfavitnogo kataloga. Dlyo nebol'shikh bibliotek* (Common rules for the description of printed material and the organisation of an alphabetic catalog. For small libraries). Moscow, Vsesoyuz kniga palata, 1963.

30 V A Vasilevskaya and E V Smirnova: (Scientific conference on cataloguing) *Sovetskaya bibliografiya,* pages 3-18, 1965 *92* (4); (Recommendations of the scientific conference on cataloguing) *Ibid,* pages 19-22.

31 Z N Ambartsumyan: in *Bibliotechnoe delo v SSSR* (Library affairs in the USSR), pages 323-340. Moscow, 1957.

32 *Desyatichnaya mezhdunarodnaya klassifikatsiya knig. Sokrashchennye tablitsy sostavlennye osoboi komissiei pri GPP dlya obyazatel'nogo upotrebleniya v bibliotekakh RSFSR* (International decimal classification of books. Abridged tables compiled by the special commission attached to the Chief Political Education Department for compulsory use in libraries of the RSFSR). Moscow, Gosizdat, 1921.

33 *Trudy pervogo Vserossiiskogo bibliograficheskogo s'ezda* (Proceedings of the first all-Russian bibliographic congress), page 70. Moscow, 1926.

34 *Ibid,* page 66.

35 *Ibid,* page 92.

36 D Balika: *Krasnyi bibliotekar,* page 46. 1924 (8).

37 *Krasnyi bibliotekar,* page 72. 1928 (1).

38 L N Tropovskii: *Desyatichnaya klassifikatsiya. Sokrashchennye tablitsy dlya massovykh bibliotek* (Decimal classification. Abridged tables for public libraries). Moscow, second edition, 1939, third edition, 1942.

39 Z N Ambartsumyan *ed*: *Tablitsy bibliotechnoi klassifikatsii dlya oblastnykh bibliotek* (Tables of library classification for regional libraries). Moscow, 1963.

40 Basic works, devoted to the library/bibliographic classification (BBK); O P Teslenks: *Sovetskaya bibliografiya,* pages 3-15. 1963 *78* (2); V G Zemlyanskaya: *Trudy* (*Gos biblioteka SSSR imeni V I Lenina*) pages 3-14. 1963 *7; Biblioteki SSSR. Opyt raboty,* pages 104-106. 1965 *28;* I P Kondakov: in *Issledovaniya i materialy* (Investigations and materials), pages 128-140. Moscow 1965 *2;* V L Birzovich, A N Kovaleva, and E I Lesokhina: *Biblioteki SSSR, Opyt raboty,* pages 66-76; 1965 *29;* Z N Ambartsumyan: *Biblioteki SSSR, Opyt raboty,* pages 57-66. 1966 *33;* E R Sukiasyan: *Biblioteki SSSR, Opyt raboty,* pages 107-127. 1965 *28.*

41 Z N Ambartsumyan: *Biblioteki SSSR, Opyt raboty,* pages 57-66. 1966 *33.*

42 Yu I Masanov: *Teoriya i praktika bibliografii. Ukazatel literatury* (Theory and practice of bibliography. Literature indexes) *1917-1958,* pages 194-200. Moscow, Vsesoyuz kniga palata, 1960.

43 *Voprosy razrabotki mekhanizirovannoi informationno—pois-kovoi sistemy dlya tsentral'nogo spravochno—informatsionnogo fonda po khimii i khimicheskoi promyshlennosti* (Problems in the development of a mechanical information search system for a central dictionary stock of information on chemistry and chemical technology), page 4. Moscow, Niitekhim, 1965.

44 *Ibid,* page 91.

45 *See* V A Vasilevskaya: *Sovetskaya bibliografiya,* pages 44-50. 1961 *66* (2); E A Novikova: *Ibid,* pages 51-71.

46 Particulars necessary for cataloguing given in published material. Inter-republic technical conditions, 29, pages 2601-66. Moscow, Kniga, second edition, 1967.

47 In this document it is stipulated that, in published children's and artistic literature and books on art, the copy of the annotated catalogue card need not be inserted if this does not correspond with the design of the artistic formulation of the publication (page 17).

This bibliography is intended to bring together the more easily accessible translations into English of Soviet papers and documents in librarianship. It has been limited to translations of complete papers and does not list the substantial body of Soviet material abstracted in English since 1967 in *Abstract journal—scientific and technical information* and the lesser body included in *Library and information science abstracts* (formerly *Library science abstracts*) since 1950.

Similarly no attempt has been made to extract the portions dealing with libraries from accounts of individual institutions such as academies of science or from general statistical returns. Papers describing techniques of information retrieval without dealing with Soviet practice and in general accounts written by Soviet authors for non-Soviet publications such as *Unesco bulletin for libraries* and *Libri* are also excluded.

The majority of the translations have been prepared by government agencies and issued as report literature. All those bearing AD, JPRS, NLL-M, NLL-RTS, NRC, PB, RAND and TT designations are normally available from the National Lending Library at Boston Spa, often as microfiche. Those noted as National Translations Center (US) are available for purchase only from the Centre at the John Crerar Library in Chicago.

GENERAL SOURCES : —

LENIN, V I: *Complete works*. The English translation of the 4th edition is being issued in Moscow and London. Lawrence and Wishart 1960-, volume and page numbers unfortunately do not correspond with the references to the Russian edition quoted throughout the present work. These references have been left as they appear in the original work. The English edition is arranged chronologically and contains writings and speeches but not decrees signed by Lenin unless the draft had been written by him. Some relevant decrees signed by him and papers by him, Krupskaia and others appear in SIMSOVA, S *editor*: *Lenin, Krupskaia and libraries,* Bingley, 1968 which is largely a translation of part of KRUPSKAIA,

173

N K: *Lenin on libraries,* Moscow, 1960. Where possible cross references between Simsova and the present work have been noted.

HORECKY, P L: *Libraries and bibliographical centers in the Soviet Union.* Indiana University publications. Slavic and East European series, volume 16 1959, contains in its supplement the text of a number of Statutes of the Lenin Library in addition to the decree listed below.

ACADEMY OF SCIENCES, USSR. LIBRARY

ANON: Libraries of the Academy of Sciences, USSR *Handbook.* Extract giving name, address, telephone, size of holdings. Translated from original. NLL *translations bulletin 3* (5) 1961, pages 395-428.

CHEBOTAREV, G A: 240 years of the library of the Academy of Sciences USSR. Translated from *Vestnik, Akademii Nauk SSSR 24* (12) 1954, pages 85-89. NLL RT 2952.

LUPPOV, S P: On the long-term plan of work of the Library of the USSR Academy of Sciences for 1966-1970. Translated from *Sovetskaya bibliografiya 96* (2) 1966, pages 107-112. NLL translations bulletin *9* (4) 1967, pages 331-342.

SCIENTIFIC CONFERENCE, LIBRARY OF THE ACADEMY OF SCIENCES, USSR. 7th Moscow, April 1961. *Proceedings: Problems of the international exchange of publications,* edited by V Ya Khvatov. Translated from original AD 607 854; TT 64 71638.

BIBLIOGRAPHY

CHERNENKO, I S: Bibliographical work in libraries of the Academies of Science of Soviet Republics. Translated from *Sovetskaya bibliografiya* (1) 1967, pages 7-13. NLL translations bulletin *9* (11) 1967, pages 1163-77.

EGOROV, P I and LYUTOVA, K V: The organisation of bibliographical work for the acquisition of foreign stocks in scientific libraries. Translated from *Sovetskaya bibliografiya* (3) 1959, pages 25-34. LLU (NLL) translations bulletin *2* (2) 1960, pages 134-49.

GASTFER, M P: Bibliography as an aid to industrial production. Translated from *Sovetskaya bibliografiya* (6) 1959, pages 10-21. NLL M 4799.

GOL'DGAMER, G I: Bibliographical information work, an important

174

stage in scientific research. Translated from *Sovetskaya bibliografiya* (5) 1959, pages 11-27. LLU (NLL) translations bulletin 2 (5) 1959, pages 387-417.

LUPPOV, S P: The Soviet bibliography of literature of natural sciences during 50 years (1917-1967). Translated from *Sovetskaya bibliografiya 103* 1967, pages 74-90. NLL RTS 4655.

MEDVEDEVA, S G and SOKOLOV, M V: Training bibliographers for scientific and technical libraries. Translated from *Sovetskaya bibliografiya* (1) 1960, pages 50-53. LLU (NLL) translations bulletin 2 (6) 1960, pages 507-512.

UNKNOWN: General bibliography—textbook for library institutes pages 183-209, General outline of the development of Soviet bibliography. Translated from *Obshchaya bibliografiya—uchebnik dlya bibliotechnykh institutov,* 1957. AD 255 416.

CLASSIFICATION AND CATALOGUING

ANON: The approval of basic order of the Soviet library classification. Translated from *Sovetskaya bibliografiya* (3) 1959, pages 102-104. LLU (NLL) translations bulletin 2 (2) 1960, pages 129-133.

KORSUNSKAYA, G V: Principles used in constructing a rubricator (subject classification for indexing) for all abstract journals of the USSR. Translated from *Nauchno-tekhnicheskaya informatsiya* series 2 (10) 1967, pages 3-5. National Translations Center (US).

KRIEGER, F J: The Soviet classification scheme for literature. Translated from introductions to various Soviet bibliographical sources 1962. RAND memorandum RM 3325 *p*R.

LIPKIN, S A and others: Modernization of traditional card catalogs by the use of microphotocopying. Translated from *Nauchno-tekhnicheskaya informatsiya* (7) 1963, pages 9-11. JPRS 21,695; TT 63 41048.

MOLODTSOV, I V: Problems of library classification. Translated from *Vestnik, Akademii Nauk SSSR* (9) 1958, pages 122-123, LLU (NLL) translations bulletin *1* (1) 1959, pages 5-7.

SHAMURIN, Ye I: Universal Decimal Classification—abbreviated tables. Translated from Russian original, Moscow 1962. JPRS 37 284.

SHUBSKAYA, L S: Sessions of Interdepartmental Commission on Classification. Translated from *Nauchno tekhnicheskaya informatsiya* (1) 1965, page 17. JPRS 31 175.

FIRSOV, G G: The Krupskaia State Library Institute (School of Librarianship) Leningrad. Translated from *Sovetskaya bibliografia* (52) 1958, pages 4-11. *Library association record 64* (11) 1962, pages 411-414.

POLUSHKIN, V A: Raising the qualifications of scientific information personnel (from experience gained in the All-Union Institute of Scientific and Technical Information). Translated from *Nauchno-tekhnicheskaya informatsiya* (1) 1963, pages 14-17. JPRS 20,592; TT 63 31502.

SKRYPNEV, N P: On the state of library education in the USSR and the means of improving it. Translated from *Sovetskaya bibliografia* (5) 1962, pages 3-9. *Journal of education for librarianship 5* (2) 1964, pages 110-113.

INFORMATION WORK IN GENERAL

ANON: Information retrieval and reproduction. Translated from *Vestnik, Akademii Nauk SSSR 35* (1) 1965, pages 133-135. JPRS 30183; TT 65 31046.

ANON: Measures for improving scientific and technical information and propaganda. Translated from *Promyshlenno-ekonomicheskaya gazeta* (58) 1959, pages 2 and 4. LLU (NLL) translations bulletin *1* (9) 1959, pages 6-11.

ANON: On activity of the All-Union Scientific and Technical Information Centre. Translated from *Sravkl konsul'tatsil retsenzii 1* (4) 1968, pages 20-22. AD 686 987.

ANUCHIN, M: A compass in the ocean of knowledge to expedite the reorganization of the scientific and technical information system. Translated from *Izvestiya,* 3 March 1964, page 4, TT 64 13948.

ARUTYUNOV, N B: Further development of the scientific and technical information system in the USSR. Translated from *Nauchno-tekhnicheskaya informatsiya,* series 1 (11) 1967, pages 3-12. PB 178 664-T.

ARUTYUNOV, N B: Construction of a single and united system of scientific and technical information. Translated from *Ekonomicheskaya gazeta* (13) 1967, pages 13-14. JPRS 40 871, TT 67 31513.

BESSKIY, K A and MARCHEVSKIY, M M: Review competition for best setup of information work in Ukrainian SSR construction industry. Translated from *Nauchno tekhnicheskaya informatsiya* (4) 1965, page 22. JPRS 31 175.

BORODIN, P I: Concerning the work of the technical information bureau of the Barnaul Radio Plant. Translated from *Nauchno tekhnicheskaya informatsiya* (8) 1966, pages 16-17 JPRS 39 141, pages 31-35; TT 66 35564.

FAYNZIGER, S S and STAROBINSKAYA, N G: Conference of leaders of information organs of RSFSR Sovnarkhozes. Translated from *Nauchno tekhnicheskaya informatsiya* (1) 1965, pages 18-19. JPRS 31 175.

FOMIN, A A: The All-Union Institute of Scientific and Technical Information and its immediate tasks. Translated from *Sovetskaya bibliografiya* (5) 1959, pages 3-10. LLU (NLL) translations bulletin *2* (4) 1960, pages 302-315.

FONOTOV, G P: On the problem of the interrelation of scientific information with bibliography and library science. Translated from *Sovetskaya bibliografiya 93* (5) 1965, pages 28-38. NLL translations bulletin *8* (8) 1966, pages 670-691.

GAUKHIN, L A and STROMILOV, N: Developments in the organisation of scientific and technical information. Translated from *Nauchne doklady vysshei shkoly filososkie nauki 8* (1) 1965, pages 3-7. JPRS 29328; TT 65 30606.

GERST, B: Technical progress and information. Translated from *Leningradskaya pravda* 4 January 1967, page 2. JPRS 39 944; TT 67 30592.

GOL'DGAMER, B I: Information and bibliographic work in the scientific research organization. Translated from *Sovetskaya bibliografiya* (52) 1958, pages 65-73. JPRS 6633.

IL'CHENKO, G V: Information and bibliographical work of TSNTB po Stroitel'stvu i Arkhitekture (Central Scientific and Technical Library for Building and Architecture). Translated from *Sovetskaya bibliografia* (6) 1961, pages 20-25. NLL translations bulletin *3* (6) 1961, pages 504-517.

KANTSLERIS, A: Exhibition of the information services of Lithuania at the Exhibition of the Achievements of the National Economy of the USSR. Translated from *Nauchno tekhnicheskaya informatsiya* (12) 1966, pages 12-14. NLL translations bulletin *9* (7) 1967, pages 708-716.

KAPTASHOV, N S and PACHEVSKII, T M: The role of libraries in the scientific information system. Translated from *Sovetskaya bibliografiya* (4) 1967, pages 23-31. NLL translations bulletin *10* (5) 1968, pages 498-516.

KOSTYANOY, G F: The role of the scientific-technical community in information work. Translated from *Nauchno tekhnicheskaya informatsiya* (6) 1966, pages 6-7 JPRS 38,453, pages 11-16; TT 66 34879.

KOTEL'NIKOV, YU B: Experience of the Kuzbasski Sovnarhoz in mechanisation of reference/information work. Translated from *Byulleten tekhniko-ekonomisheskoi informatsii* (8) 1963, pages 68-70. JPRS 22 135; TT 63 41291.

KOTLYAREVSKII, B Z: An analysis of ways and means of improving the economic effectiveness of scientific information in the USSR food industry. Translated from *Nauchno tekhnicheskaya informatsiya* series 1 (6) 1967, pages 8-9. National Translations Center (US).

KREMENETSKAYA, A V and others: Organisation of scientific information (in the USSR). Translated from *Vestnik, Akademii Nauk SSSR 22* (8/9) 1952, pages 41-45, 46-52, 81-91. NLL M 548-550; (UK) Ministry of Supply TIB/T 4271.

KRITSKAYA, Z P editor: Scientific Information Institute, Academy of Sciences of the USSR. Translated from *Institut nauchnoy informatsii Akademii nauk SSSR,* Moscow, 1963, 32 pages. JPRS 24,691; TT 64 31297.

LOBANOV, G V: Conference on improving the work of information organs of the State Committee of construction, road and communal machine building. Translated from *Nauchno tekhnicheskaya informatsiya* (4) 1965, page 21. JPRS 31 175.

LOPATKIN, L: Organisation of the scientific and technical information service in USSR. Translated from *Nauka i tekhnika* (6) 1966, pages 10-12. JRRS 39 124; TT 66 35547.

MELIK-SHAKHNAZAROV, A S: Technological information in machine building. Translated as: 'Technical information in the USSR'. Translated from original Moscow, 1960. Cambridge, Massachusetts Institute of Technology Libraries, library monographs no 3 1961, 121 pages.

MIKHAILOV, A I (*sic*): The mutual linkage of scientific information with librarianship and bibliography. Translated from *Sovetskaya bibliografia* (2) 1965, pages 6-12. NLL translations bulletin *7* (10) 1965, pages 849-863.

MIKHAYLOV, A I and others: Foundations of scientific information. Chapter 7, sections 1 and 2: the organisation of scientific and technical information in the Communist world, pages 494-544. Translated from original, Moscow, 1965. AD 627 802; TT 66 60478.

MIKHAYLOV, A I and others: The development of informatics in the USSR. Translated from *Nauchno tekhnicheskaya informatsiya,* series 2 (11) 1967, pages 3-18. PB 178 665-T.

MOROZOVA, E: Improve the propagation of technical literature. Translated from *Bibliotekar* (10) 1960, pages 5-7. NLL translations bulletin *3* (4) 1961, pages 320-327.

MOROZOVA, YE N: Technical information and bibliographical centers in the USSR and the data published by them. Translated from *Obshchestvo po rasprostraneniyu polsticheskikh i nauchnykh znaniy RSFSR,* Leningrad, 1959, pages 1-23. AD 259 239.

MOROZOVZ, E N: The organisation of a single system of scientific technical libraries in the USSR. Translated from *Sovetskaya bibliografia* (52) 1958, pages 81-83. *Library association record 64* (11) 1962, pages 415-416.

NEMETSOV, V D and MAL'CHEVSKAYA, L F: Progress in creating chemical information retrieval systems for chemical science and industry. Translated from *Khimicheskaya promyshlennost Ukrainy* (4) 1968, pages 57-60. National Translations Center (US).

OREKHOV, P M: New standard regulations on the duties and rights of scientific-technical information organisations. Translated from *Nauchno tekhnicheskaya informatsiya* (8) 1963, pages 3-5. JPRS 22,210; TT 63 41327.

PAKHOLOV, D T: The role of the information service in a large industrial enterprise. Translated from *Nauchno tekhnicheskaya informatsiya* (2) 1966, pages 5-6. JPRS 36,766 pages 7-11; TT 66 33197.

POLUBOYARINOV, M: Scientific, technical and specialist libraries in the USSR. Translated from *Vestnik statistiki* (1) 1962, pages 24-33. NLL translations bulletin *6* (6) 1964, pages 519-540. and *Library association record 66* (7) 1964, pages 291-296.

POLUSHKIN, V A: The past 10 years at VINITI (All-Union Institute of Scientific and Technical Information). Translated from *Vestnik,*

Akedemii Nauk SSSR 33 (3) 1963, pages 127-128. JPRS 19 482; TT 63 21950.

POPUSHKIN, V A: Mechanisation and automation of information work. Translated from *Vestnik, Akademii Nauk SSSR* (11) 1963, pages 82-85. NLL translations bulletin *6* (4) 1964, pages 324-329.

POTEMKIN, V: VINITI provides needed technical information service. Translated from *Kommunist 41* (3) 23 October 1964, page 3. JPRS 28385; TT 65 30167.

ROMANOV, I I: Scientific and technical information and propaganda as an aid to the mechanisation and automation of production. Translated from *Mekhanizatsiya i automatizatsiya 16* (6) 1962, pages 43-45. NLL translations bulletin *5* (1) 1963, pages 1-10.

SMIRNOV, K A and GOLANT, M E: The establishment of an information system on technical standard documentation. Translated from *Standarty i kachestvo 32* (1) 1968, pages 68-70. NLL Translations Bulletin, *10* (10) 1968, pages 1141-51 NLL RTS 4865.

USSR COUNCIL OF MINISTERS Decree 1185, 25 June 1955. Measures for improving the use of scientific and technical literature, patents and catalogues of foreign countries. Translated from Russian original.

HORECKY, P L: *Libraries and bibliographic centres in the Soviet Union*. Indiana University Publications, Slavic and East European series Vol 16 1959, pages 234-239.

VOYTSIKOV, B N: Functions of territorial interbranch information agencies. Translated from *Nauchno tekhnicheskaya informatsiya* (1) 1967, pages 9-11. JPRS 40606 pages 13-19; TT 67 31250.

ZADERMAN, L and KOLOKOLOVA, O: A state information system. Translated from *Bibliotekar* (5) 1967, pages 4-7. NLL translations bulletin *9* (10) 1967, pages 1046-56.

LIBRARIES

ANON: A list of libraries. Translated from *Informatsionnyy ukazatel' bibliograficheskikh spiskov i kartotek* (9) 1961, pages 26-30. JPRS 4913; TT 61 28071.

ANON: Reference publications of the Lenin State Library of the USSR. Translated from *Bibliotekar* (10) 1958, pages 60-61. LLU (NLL) translations bulletin *1* (2) 1959, pages 41-44. NLL M 606.

AGRANOVSKII, V: Secrets of the Patent Library. Translated from *Ekonomicheskaya gazeta*, (3) 1961, pages 21-22. TT 61-28370.

KOLOBOVA, N: The reader's information service (Central Poly-technical Library, Moscow). Translated from *Bibliotekar* (10) 1960, pages 7-9. National research Council of Canada, Technical Translation 946.

MOROZOV, A M: Medical libraries in the Soviet Union. Translated from *Sovetskoe zdravookhranenie 24* (6) 1965, pages 51-54. NLL RTS 3817.

MOROSOV, A N: Certain questions of the functioning of the USSR Patent Library. Translated from *Nauchno tekhnicheskaya informatsiya* (8) 1966, pages 3-6. JPRS 39 141 pages 1-9; TT 66 35564.

MORACHEVSKII, N I: Guide to the M E Saltykov-Shchedrin State Public Library Leningrad. Translated from Russian original dated 1956. University of California, Los Angeles, Library Occasional Papers, number 14, 1963.

PROPOSED PLANS

ANON: Plan for scientific research work in the field of scientific/technical information for 1964-1965. Translated from *Nauchno tekhnicheskaya informatsiya* (7) 1963, pages 3-4. JPRS 21695; TT 63 41048; NLL *translations bulletin 6* (1) 1964, pages 53-59.

ANON: Results of work in 1965 and tasks for the information organs in 1966. Translated from *Nauchno tekhnicheskaya informatsiya* (1) 1966, pages 3-5. JPRS 36 765 pages 1-9; TT 66 33196.

ANON: Principal tasks of information agencies in 1967. Translated from *Nauchno tekhnicheskaya informatsiya* (1) 1967, pages 3-5. JPRS 40606 pages 1-4; TT 67 31250.

STANDARDS FOR LIBRARY WORK

KAYDAROVICH, V I: Pilot organisation for standardisation in the area of scientific and technical information. Translated from *Nauchno tekhnicheskaya informatsiya* (1) 1967, pages 6-7. JPRS 40606 pages 5-9; TT 67 31250.

RABEI, M: Norms in library work. Translated from *Bibliotekar* (10) 1958, pages 43-46. LLU (NLL) translations bulletin *1* (2) 1959, pages 44-48; NLL translation M 612; TT 59-22636.

TRANSLATIONS WORK

MALYARENKO, D: Experiment in organizing the translation of foreign literature at ' the Giproniselektroshakht Institute '. Translated from *Nauchno tekhnicheskaya informatsiya* (3) 1963, page 12. TT 66 13809.

VLADYCHENKO, V V: The system of coordination of translations in the USSR. Translated from *Tekhnicheskie biblioteki SSSR 30* (8) 1964, pages 3-7. TT 66 20987.

Writings by non-Soviet authors on Soviet libraries abound and a bibliography would obviously be a major undertaking. Apart from the normal sources such as *Library and information science abstracts, Library literature,* etc, the works by Horecky — noted above — as well as Ruggles, M J and Swank, R C; *Soviet libraries and librarianship,* Chicago, American Library Association, 1962 and Whatley H A and Wilson T D; *A British view of libraries in the USA and the USSR,* Association of Assistant Librarians, 1967 all contain bibliographies which may be particularly useful when starting a study based on the non-Soviet viewpoint.